HOW DO DINOSAURS RULE THE EARTH

YOUR FEEDBACK MATTERS TO US

Welcome to the world of dinosaurs and the interactive experience with **DINOAR3D!** As you dive into the pages of this book and explore prehistoric times, we hope you enjoy every discovery, each species, and the 3D animations.

When you finish reading, we invite you to leave us a **review on Amazon**. Your feedback helps us improve and create more interactive and educational content. We'd love to hear which parts of the book you enjoyed most, your experience with augmented reality, and any details you found interesting or helpful.

Thank you for joining us on this prehistoric adventure and for helping us grow with your feedback!

INSTRUCTIONS FOR USING THE DINOAR3D APP

1. Download the DINOAR3D app

Find the DINOAR3D application in your device's app store and download it. The app is compatible with mobile devices and tablets.

2. Point the camera at the statistics section

With the app open, aim your device's camera at the dinosaur's statistics section in the book. Make sure the camera captures the image well so the dinosaur appears on the screen.

3. Watch the dinosaur in action

Once properly focused, you will see the high-quality dinosaur appear. You can watch it move its head and tail, waiting for a command.

4. Family interaction with the action buttons

The app includes three action buttons that allow the whole family—both parents and children—to interact with the dinosaur. Each button activates different movements or sounds, creating a fun and educational experience.

4. Explore and have fun

Enjoy watching the dinosaur respond to your commands and exploring the various available actions. It's a great opportunity to learn and have fun together as a family!

Note: Make sure your device has enough battery, good lighting for better image recognition, and a stable connection to enjoy the best experience.

CONTENTS

DEDICATION

To all the young adventurers,

May your imaginations soar as high as the pterosaurs and your curiosity roam as far as the mighty sauropods. This book is for you, with the hopes that it ignites a lifelong love for learning and a passion for exploring the wonders of our prehistoric past.

I hope you enjoy this beginner's crash course on dinosaurs!

Chemak Publish

A TRIP TO PREHISTORY: WELCOME TO THE WORLD OF DINOSAURS

Did you know that if the first dinosaur born were alive today, it would be around 230 million years old? I know what you're thinking; that's a lot of birthdays— and you're right!

When dinosaurs roamed the planet, the Earth was a very different place than what you and I know. Today, we live on one of seven continents: Africa, Antarctica, Asia, Europe, North America, Australia, and South America.

But, when dinosaurs were here, there was only one continent— Pangea. That's right, all seven continents on Earth were part of one big mass of land. So if a dinosaur wanted to take a jog from Hawaii to New Zealand, they could have— energy permitting, of course.

We all know that dinosaurs were giant reptiles that lived on Earth before us, but what does the word dinosaur mean? The name actually translates to terrible lizard, and they came in all shapes and sizes. Some dinosaurs were as small as chickens, while others were bigger than elephants! Scientists believe dinosaurs are related to today's crocodiles, snakes, lizards, and birds.

TIME OF THE DINOSAURS

Since we already covered how different Earth was back in the time of dinosaurs, lets look at the periods in which they lived. Most people think that these giant creatures roamed the planet together at the same time, but that wasn't the case. To best understand these periods, lets think of them like chapters of a book.

The story of the dinosaurs begins during the Precambrian period, which started when Earth formed and lasted until about 542 million years ago. This is when life was just getting started, but it wasn't until the next chapter, called the Paleozoic Era, that things really got going.

The Paleozoic Era lasted from 542 to 250 million years ago and had lots of exciting moments, like when multicellular life first appeared.

The Paleozoic Era has a few chapters to it: The Cambrian period, the Ordovician, the Silurian, the Devonian, the Carboniferous, and finally the Permian. Each of these periods had its own cast of unique characters and stories.

After the Paleozoic Era came the Mesozoic Era, which lasted from 250 to 65 million years ago. This era is often called the age of dinosaurs because it's when they ruled the Earth. The Mesozoic Era is divided into three chapters: the Triassic, Jurassic, and Cretaceous periods.

These periods were full of fantastic creatures, including most of the famous dinosaurs that we see in movies and TV shows today. I'm sure you've all heard of the tyrannosaurus rex or a raptor before.

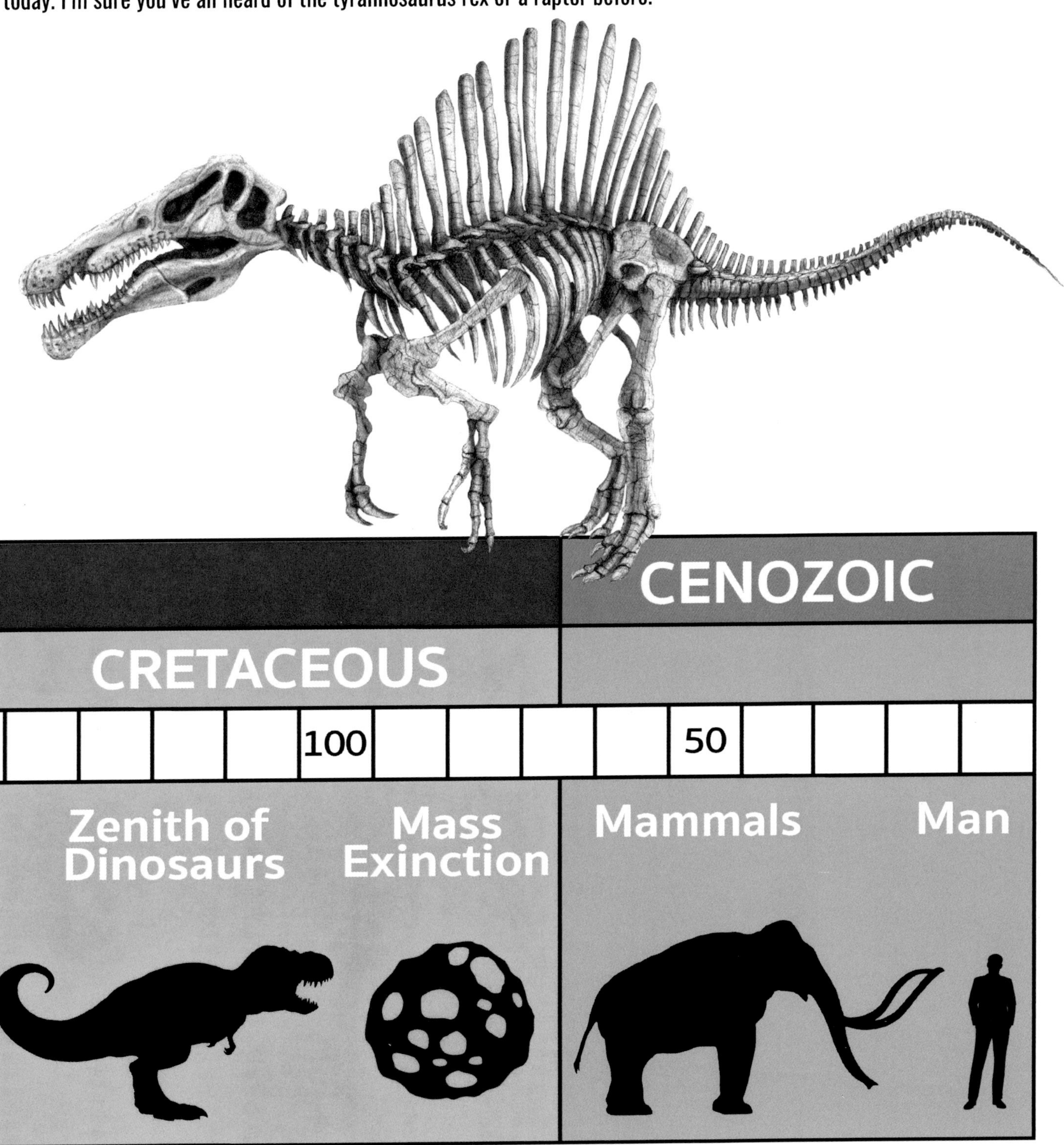

Fun Facts about the T-Rex

- Land Animals: Archosaurs and therapsids (mammal-like reptiles).
- Marine Animals: Plesiosaurs, ichthyosaurs (like big swimming lizards), and fish
- Avian Animals: None mentioned
- Plant Life: Cycads (similar to palm trees), ferns, Gingko-like trees, and seed plants

Jurassic Period (201–145 million years ago)

- Land Animals: Dinosaurs (like sauropods and therapods), early mammals, and some feathered dinosaurs
- Marine Animals: Plesiosaurs, ichthyosaurs (like big swimming lizards), and fish

- Avian Animals: None mentioned
- Plant Life: Cycads (similar to palm trees), ferns, Gingko-like trees, and seed plants

Cretaceous Period (145–66 million years ago)

- Land Animals: Dinosaurs (like sauropods, therapods, raptors, and herbivorous ceratopsians), plus small mammals living in trees
- Marine Animals: Plesiosaurs, pliosaurs, mosasaurs (like giant sea lizards), sharks, fish, squid, and other aquatic reptiles
- Avian Animals: Pterosaurs, some flying insects, and feathered birds
- Plant Life: This period saw a massive growth in flowering plants, along with ferns, conifers, cycads, and other plants.

Each period had its own unique cast of characters, from mighty dinosaurs to ancient plants, and they all played a part in shaping the Earth as we know it today!

FLORA, FAUNA, AND MORE

In this section, we'll take a slightly deeper look into each of the three major periods and explore the plants and animals in more detail.

Fun Facts about the T-Rex

The Triassic period started 250 million years ago, just after a big disaster called the Permian/Triassic Extinction, which wiped out lots of animals. This period saw the rise of new creatures like dinosaurs and the first mammals.

Where it Happened:

All the continents were joined together in a supercontinent called Pangaea, surrounded by a vast ocean called Panthalassa. It was sweltering in the middle, with lots of rain. The north and south were wetter.

What Lived There:

- Land Animals: Reptiles became dominant, with early dinosaurs like Eoraptor appearing. Some reptiles evolved into pterosaurs (like flying reptiles) and crocodiles. Small mammals also started to appear.
- Marine Life: After the big extinction, new aquatic reptiles like ichthyosaurs and plesiosaurs took over the oceans. There were also big fish and simple creatures like corals.
- Plant Life: The land wasn't as green as in later periods, but there were still plants like cycads and ferns. There wasn't enough food for giant plant-eating animals like dinosaurs yet.

The End of the Triassic:

The Triassic period ended with another smaller extinction event, which wiped out some marine reptiles and large amphibians. We're not sure exactly what caused it, but it might have been volcanoes or a meteor.

In the Triassic, Earth was recovering from disaster, and new creatures were starting to take over, setting the stage for the age of dinosaurs to come!

The Jurassic Period

In the time of the Jurassic, which is famous thanks to movies like Jurassic Park, dinosaurs ruled the Earth. This period marked the rise of huge sauropods like Brachiosaurus and meat-eating theropods like Allosaurus.

- Fun Fact!: What's a theropod, you ask? A theropod is a type of carnivorous dinosaur that walks on two legs and has short forelimbs. Examples are Tyrannosaurus Rex and Velociraptor. They have hollow bones and typically three toes on each limb. In fact, birds are believed to be descended from one lineage of small theropods!

Where it Happened:

The supercontinent Pangaea broke apart during the Jurassic, forming two big pieces called Gondwana in the south and Laurasia in the north. Lakes and rivers formed, creating new homes for animals.

What Lived There:

- Dinosaurs: Small dinosaurs evolved into giants like Brachiosaurus. Meat-eaters like Allosaurus hunted them.
- Mammals: Tiny mammals stayed hidden from dinosaurs. The first feathered dinosaurs appeared, but birds didn't fully evolve yet.
- Marine Life: Huge sea reptiles ruled the oceans like Liopleurodon and Elasmosaurus.
- Avian Life: The skies were filled with flying reptiles called pterosaurs.
- Plant Life: Thick forests covered the land, with ferns, conifers, and other plants providing food for the giant dinosaurs.

In the Jurassic, life on Earth was enormous, from the towering dinosaurs to the lush forests they roamed!

The Cretaceous Period

Then came the Cretaceous period— a time when dinosaurs were everywhere! There were lots of different kinds, from big meat-eaters to plant-eaters with horns and armor.

Where it Happened:

The supercontinent Pangaea was breaking apart, and the continents we know today were forming. It was hot and wet in many places, with lots of swamps.

What Lived There:

- Dinosaurs: This was the heyday of dinosaurs. There were all kinds, from raptors to huge, long-necked sauropods. They roamed the land, with some even flying above.
- Mammals: Mammals were still around but mostly kept hidden from the big dinosaurs. Some, like Repenomamus, were big enough to eat baby dinosaurs.
- Marine Life: The oceans were ruled by giant reptiles like mosasaurs and pliosaurs. Fish and sharks were also common.
- Avian Life: Pterosaurs ruled the skies at first, but then birds started to appear, evolving from feathered dinosaurs.

Plant Life: Flowering plants were spreading quickly, along with thick forests and other greenery. This fed the dinosaurs and helped insects like beetles thrive.

The End of the Cretaceous:

The Cretaceous period ended with a big bang when a meteor hit Earth, causing dust to block out the sun. This killed off most plants, which meant no food for plant-eating dinosaurs. Without them, even the meat-eaters couldn't survive, making way for mammals to take over in the next period.

In the Cretaceous, dinosaurs ruled the land, sea, and sky until a dramatic end changed the course of Earth's history.

DINO DIETS:
THE THREE MAIN TYPES OF DINOSAURS

We all like to eat, right? Well, the dinosaurs were no different. While you may have a ton of favorite foods like cereal, gummy snacks, broccoli, sushi, pizza, and cheeseburgers, our dino-pals were rather limited in options. Despite this, virtually all dinosaurs can be sorted into three primary types: carnivores, herbivores, and omnivores.

Carnivores: Carnivores were the meat-eaters of the dinosaur world. They had sharp teeth for tearing flesh and claws for catching prey. The carnivorous bunch was quite terrifying, especially if you found yourself a favorite on their menu. As for us humans, we couldn't survive healthily on meat alone, which means we wouldn't make very good carnivores.

Notable Carnivores:

- Tyrannosaurus rex
- Velociraptor
- Allosaurus
- Spinosaurus
- Giganotosaurus

Herbivores: These dinosaurs were like the plant-eaters of the dinosaur world. They had special teeth for grinding up plants and leaves. This lot of plant-eaters are generally deemed the gentle giants of the dinosaur kingdom. There are plenty of vegetarians in the world, and if you're one of them, chances are you enjoy a lot of food that these herbivores would love.

Notable Herbivores:

- Triceratops
- Stegosaurus
- Brachiosaurus
- Ankylosaurus
- Parasaurolophus

Omnivores: Omnivores were dinosaurs that ate both plants and meat. They had a mix of teeth for tearing meat and grinding plants. They could eat a variety of foods depending on what was available, making them adaptable to different environments. As for humans, a vast majority of us fall into this category, which means we have a well-rounded diet with a lot of options.

Notable Herbivores:

- Oviraptor
- Ornithomimus
- Gallimimus
- Therizinosaurus
- Baryonyx

TYRANNOSAURUS REX

Most of us are familiar with the mighty Tyrannosaurus rex, also known as T. rex— the king of the terrible lizards!

Imagine a gigantic predator, around 40 feet long, prowling through ancient forests in what is now western North America. With its keen sense of smell, it spots its next meal, a Triceratops, and swiftly gives chase.

With a standard speed of 12 miles per hour, this carnivore easily catches slow, unexpecting prey. With a single powerful bite, it's capable of ripping off a huge chunk of meat weighing over two hundred pounds! Then, in a spectacular display, it tosses the flesh high into the air, catching it skillfully to swallow it whole. – Just like in Jurassic Park, the movie (1993).

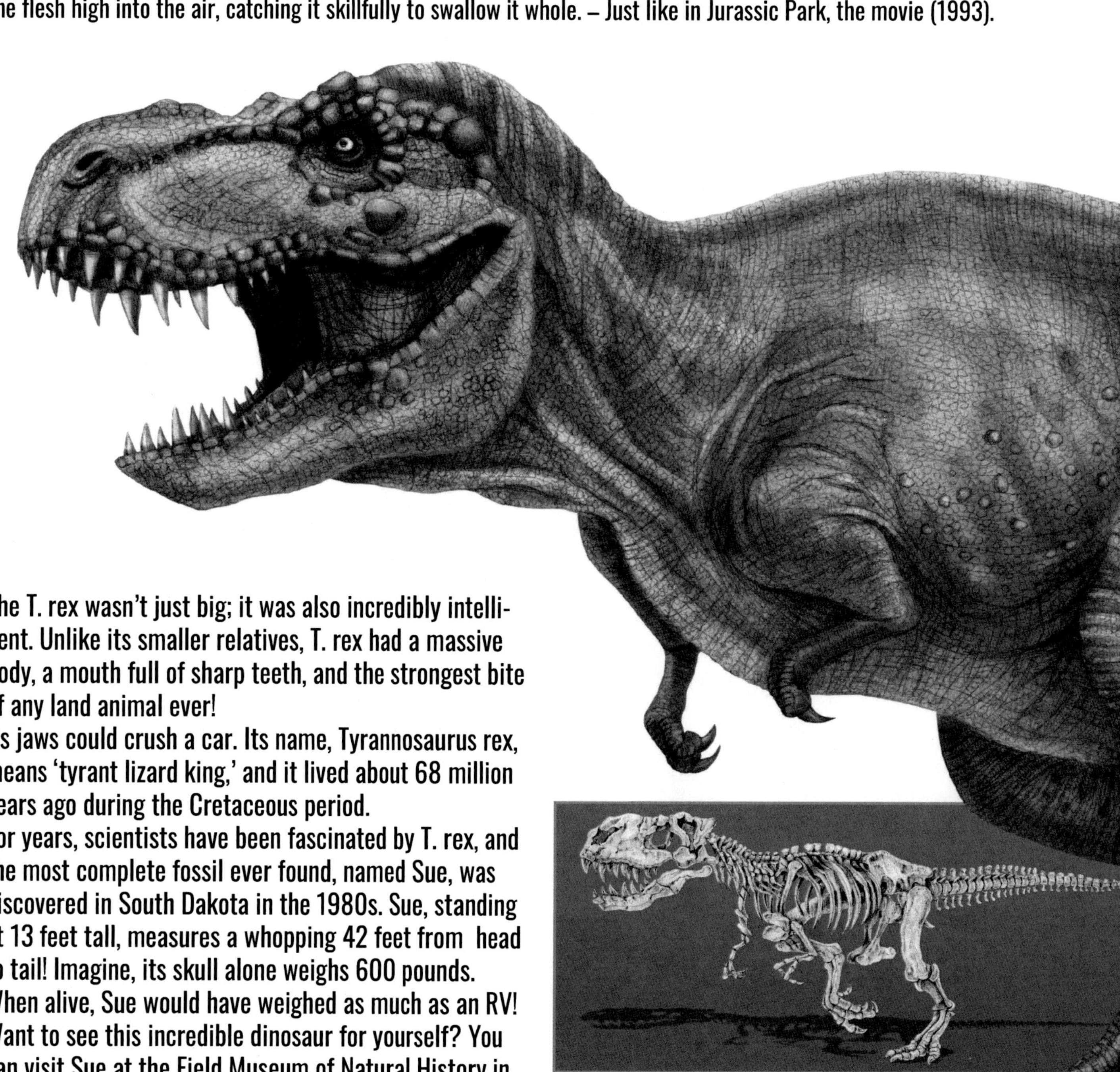

The T. rex wasn't just big; it was also incredibly intelligent. Unlike its smaller relatives, T. rex had a massive body, a mouth full of sharp teeth, and the strongest bite of any land animal ever!

Its jaws could crush a car. Its name, Tyrannosaurus rex, means 'tyrant lizard king,' and it lived about 68 million years ago during the Cretaceous period.

For years, scientists have been fascinated by T. rex, and the most complete fossil ever found, named Sue, was discovered in South Dakota in the 1980s. Sue, standing at 13 feet tall, measures a whopping 42 feet from head to tail! Imagine, its skull alone weighs 600 pounds. When alive, Sue would have weighed as much as an RV! Want to see this incredible dinosaur for yourself? You can visit Sue at the Field Museum of Natural History in Chicago, Illinois.

TYRANNOSAURUS REX

T-Rex Stats

Period: Late Cretaceous
Average Height: 15-20 feet
Average Length: 40 feet
Average Weight: 9 tons
Diet: Carnivore
Roamed: North America
Speed of about: 12-18 mph

Fun Facts about the T-Rex

1. A full-grown T-Rex could sprint up to 20 mph. For context, the fastest anyone has run (so far) is about 27 miles per hour, a speed reached (briefly) by sprinter Usain Bolt in 2009.
2. The largest T-Rex tooth ever found was twelve inches long!
3. With a mouthful of teeth the size of bananas, these amazing eaters could tear off around 200 pounds of meat in just one bite!

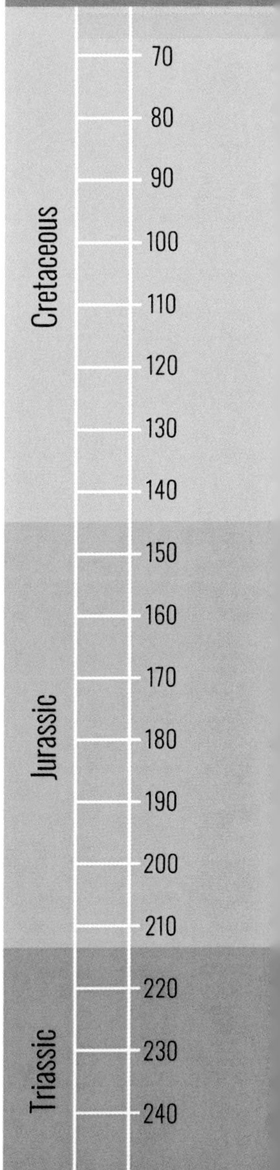

Cretaceous | Jurassic | Triassic
70 80 90 100 110 120 130 140 150 160 170 180 190 200 210 220 230 240

VELOCIRAPTOR

Velociraptors were a group of sleek and agile dinosaurs known for their speed, and they lived during the late Cretaceous period. Their name, which means 'swift thief,' perfectly describes their quick movements.

They had unique features like slightly curved skulls and claw-like sickles on their second toes they used to hunt and climb trees with. Velociraptors possessed around 80 sharp teeth, and their jaws were super strong.

Fun Facts about the Velociraptor

1. Did you know that the Velociraptor in 'Jurassic Park' is actually based on a larger, scarier dinosaur called Deinonychus antirrhopus, who lived about 30 million years before Velociraptors?
2. Velociraptors lived in the Central Asia region, not North America.
3. Another common misconception is that they hunted in packs, but it's believed they were more solitary hunters. It's entirely possible they were even capable of climbing trees to catch prey, thanks to their retractable claws.

VELOCIRAPTOR

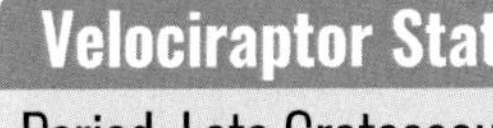

Period: Late Cretaceous
Average Height: 1.6 feet
Average Length: 6.8 feet
Average Weight: 22-45 pounds
Diet: Carnivore
Roamed: Mongolia
Speed of about: 24-34 mph

Velociraptors were small dinosaurs, about 6 feet long and 1.6 feet tall at the hip, weighing around 33 pounds, similar to a modern-day turkey. Their most striking feature was their sickle-shaped claws on their second toes, used for grabbing onto prey. Their long, low skulls and large eye sockets indicated excellent vision. They had streamlined bodies with powerful hind legs for speed and agility. Despite their short arms, their hands had three fingers with retractable claws.

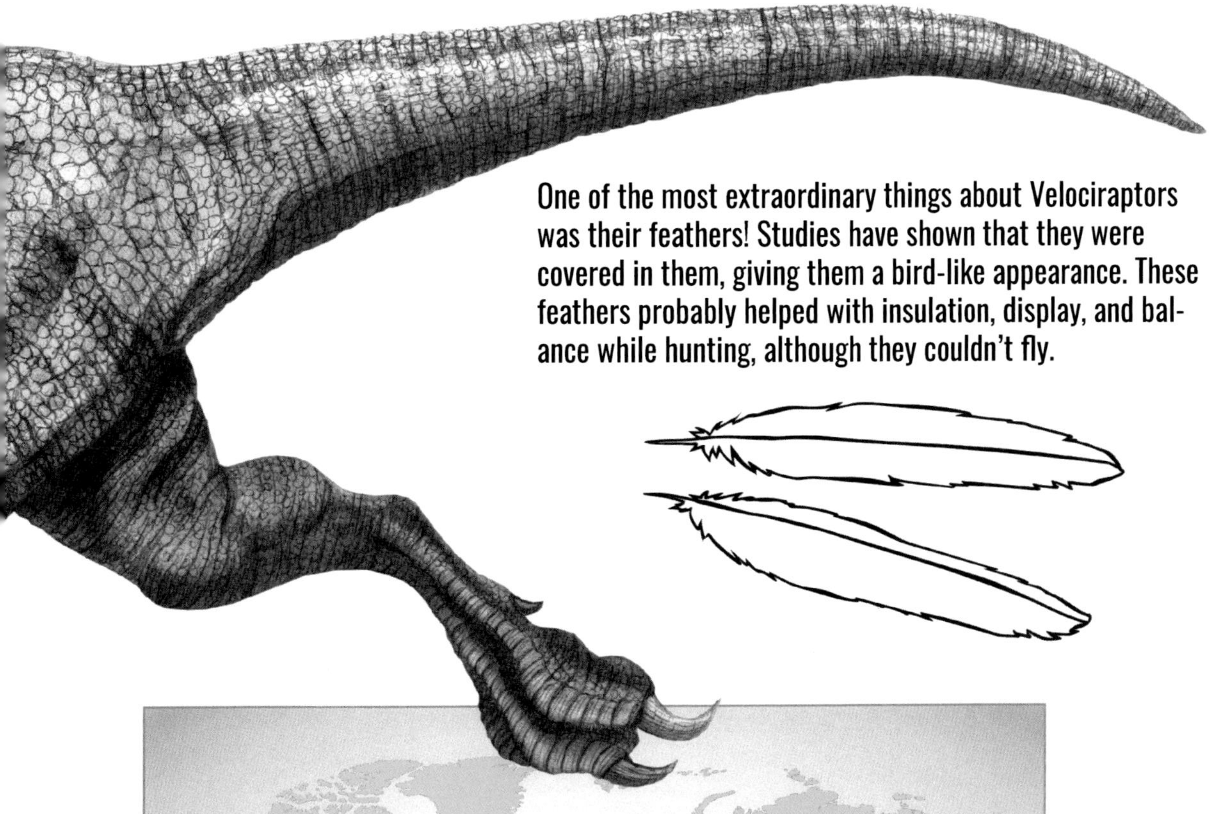

One of the most extraordinary things about Velociraptors was their feathers! Studies have shown that they were covered in them, giving them a bird-like appearance. These feathers probably helped with insulation, display, and balance while hunting, although they couldn't fly.

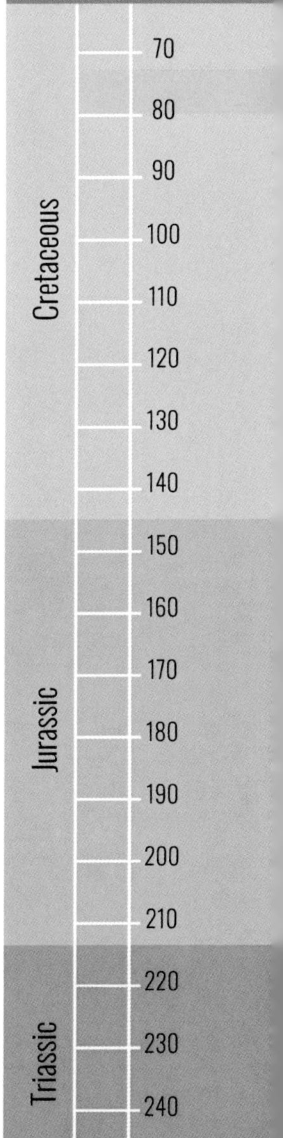

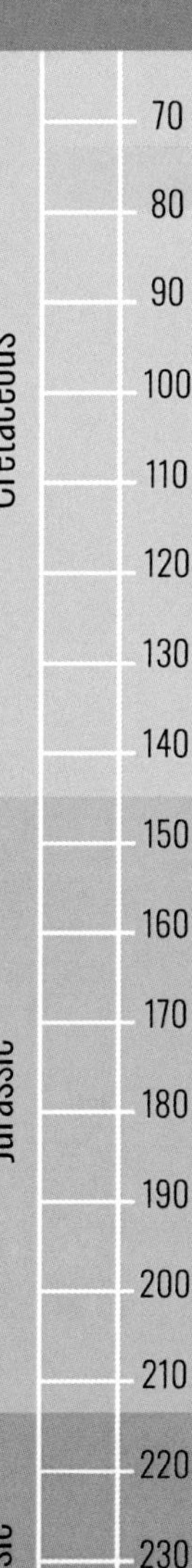

BRACHIOSAURUS

Brachiosaurus lived around 156 to 145 million years ago during the Jurassic period. It was massive, stretching over 80 feet long and weighing more than 28 tons—that's as heavy as four African elephants stacked on top of each other! Not to mention, it was as tall as a four-story building, and it's one of the largest animals ever to roam the Earth! That's around 30- 43 feet in height!

Why was it so huge? Some experts believe that Brachiosaurus couldn't run very fast, so its size most likely helped to protect it from big predators like the Allosaurus. Others think its gigantic size helped it digest tough plants better, as it needed a big belly to process all that food.

The name Brachiosaurus comes from Greek words meaning 'arm lizard' because its front legs were longer than its back legs.

This unique feature helped it reach high into the trees for its favorite snacks. Brachiosaurus was a sauropod, a family of dinosaurs known for their long necks, tails, and walking on all fours. Another famous sauropod that you may have heard of is the Apatosaurus.

Fun Facts about the Brachiosaurus

1. Scientists once believed that Brachiosaurus lived in water because of its size and the position of its nostrils; however, they later realized that being underwater would have made it hard for Brachiosaurus to breathe air.
2. It's believed that they could live to be over 100 years old!
3. Brachiosaurus had long front limbs compared to its hind limbs, giving it a posture similar to a giraffe. This helped it reach high tree branches without straining its neck, making it easier to munch on tasty leaves!

BRACHIOSAURUS

Brachiosaurus Stats

Period: Late Jurassic
Average Height: 30-40 feet
Average Length: 85 feet
Average Weight: 30-80 tons
Diet: Herbivore
Roamed: North America, Africa
Speed of about: 5 mph

Footprints of Brachiosaurus sauropod dinosaur. Valdecevillo site near ENCISO village, La Rioja, Spain.

Cretaceous
Jurassic
Triassic

70
80
90
100
110
120
130
140
150
160
170
180
190
200
210
220
230
240

DILOPHOSAURUS

Dilophosaurus means 'double-crested lizard' in Greek, which is a direct reference to this unique dino's headgear. This cool-looking lizard got its name because it had two thin, bony crests that lined the top of its head. Scientists think these crests might have been covered in a substance called keratin, which is the same material as our fingernails! They're not sure what shape the crests were, but they could have been brightly colored to impress other dinos, kind of like fancy hats!

Paleontologists discovered that Dilophosaurus had air pockets in its bones, making its skeleton strong but light. This allowed Dilophosaurus to grow bigger than other dinosaurs at the time, weighing around 1,500 pounds! When Dilophosaurus roamed North America during the Jurassic period, about 195 million years ago, it was one of the fiercest predators around.

However, about 50 million years later, another dinosaur called the Allosaurus became the top predator. And then, 77 million years after that, the mighty Tyrannosaurus rex took the top spot! Dinosaurs sure had a lot of competition for being on top of the food chain.

Dilophosaurus

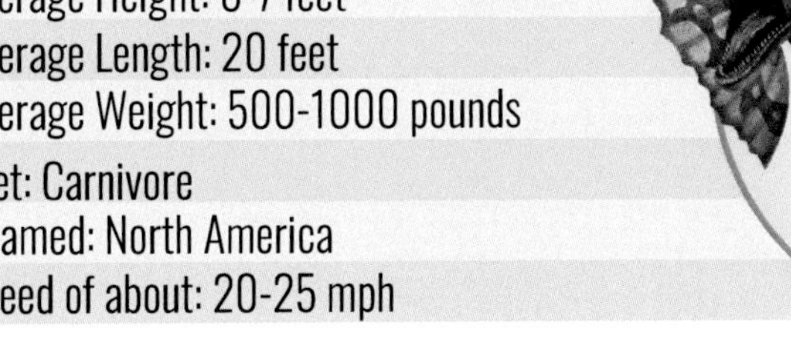

Period: Early Jurassic
Average Height: 6-7 feet
Average Length: 20 feet
Average Weight: 500-1000 pounds
Diet: Carnivore
Roamed: North America
Speed of about: 20-25 mph

Fun Facts about the Brachiosaurus

1. Did you know there's no evidence that this dinosaur was poisonous or could spray venom like in the movies?
2. Another movie myth busted: these dinosaurs didn't have expandable neck frills like they showed in films.
3. While the movies would have us believe these were small dinosaurs, the truth was they could get as long as 20 feet!

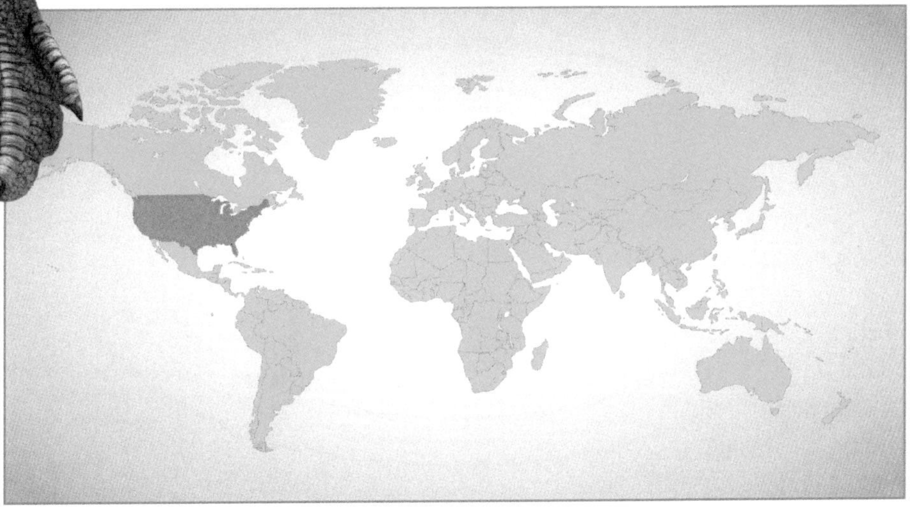

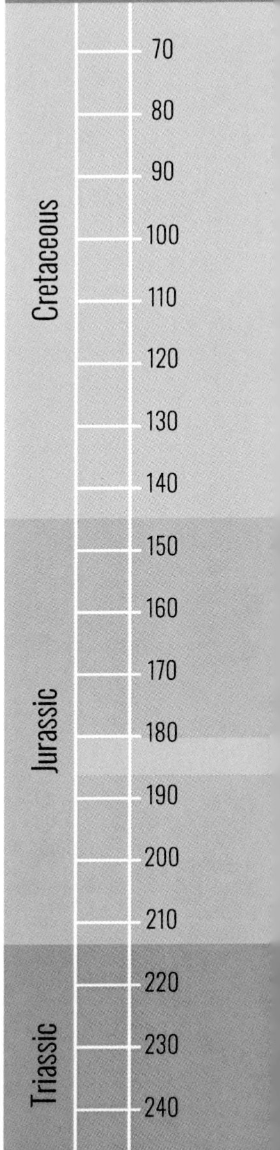

DILOPHOSAURUS

DILOPHOSAURUS

The Triceratops, which literally means 'three-horned face' in Greek, is a well-known herbivorous dinosaur that roamed the Earth during the Cretaceous period, primarily inhabiting regions of North America. Its fossils have been unearthed in various locations, including North Dakota, Wyoming, and Saskatchewan in Canada.

Easily recognizable, the Triceratops boasted three distinct horns on its head, situated beneath an armored crest shielding its neck and shoulders.

This massive creature moved on all fours, relying on plant-based diets for sustenance. While its formidable horns may appear menacing, researchers speculate they were primarily utilized for defense and display rather than for hunting live prey.

Interestingly, some scientists propose that the horns of Triceratops served more as tools for mating rituals and intimidating rivals rather than as weapons for combat.

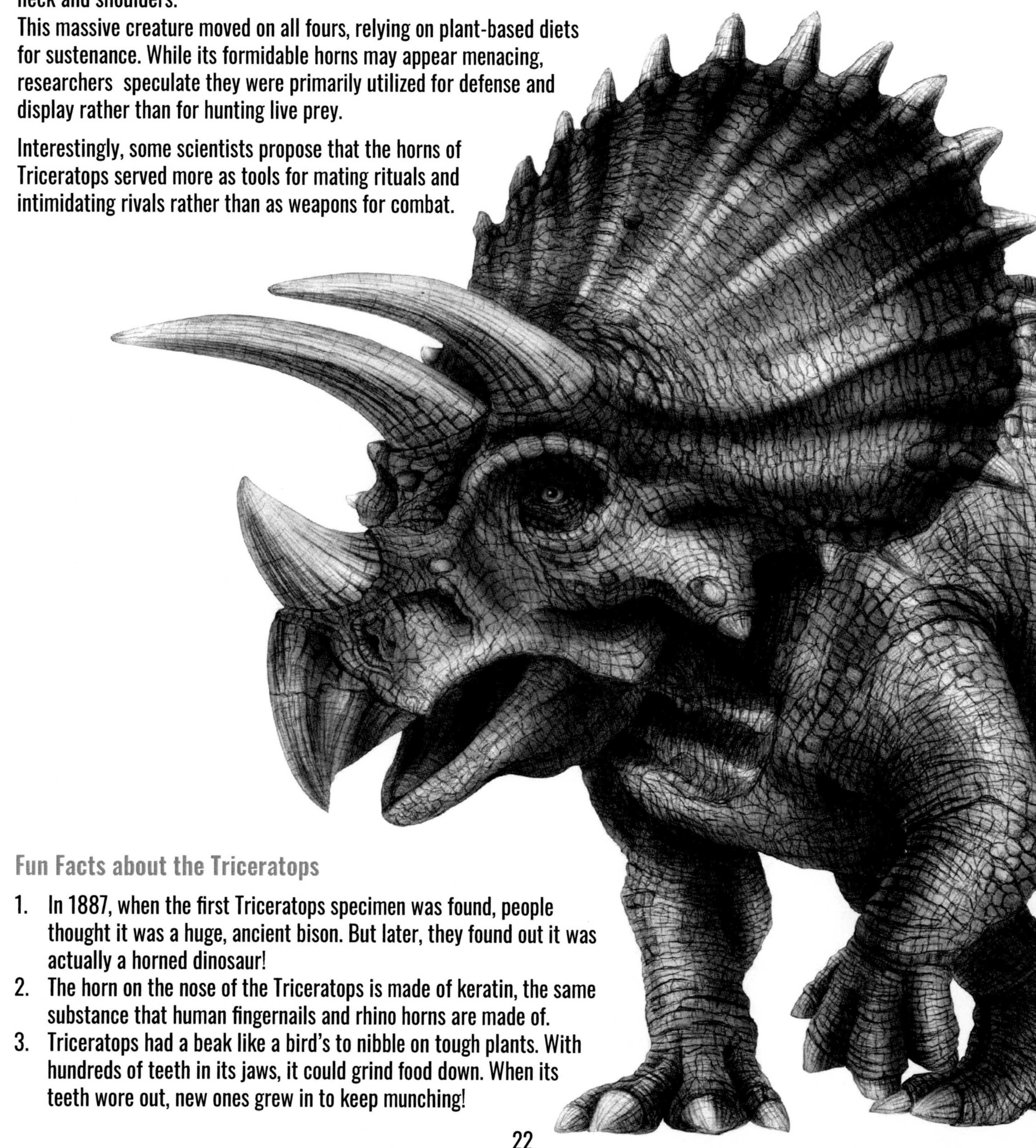

Fun Facts about the Triceratops

1. In 1887, when the first Triceratops specimen was found, people thought it was a huge, ancient bison. But later, they found out it was actually a horned dinosaur!
2. The horn on the nose of the Triceratops is made of keratin, the same substance that human fingernails and rhino horns are made of.
3. Triceratops had a beak like a bird's to nibble on tough plants. With hundreds of teeth in its jaws, it could grind food down. When its teeth wore out, new ones grew in to keep munching!

Triceratops Stats

Period: Late Cretaceous
Average Height: 9-10 feet
Average Length: 26-30 feet
Average Weight: 6-12 tons
Diet: Herbivore
Roamed: North America
Speed of about: 15-20 mph

TRICERAPTOS

Due to their low-slung heads, the Triceratops likely fed on low-growing vegetation, but their horns, beak, and size may have enabled them to knock down taller plants. Their jaws featured a deep, narrow beak, which is thought to have been more adept at grasping and plucking food rather than biting it.

Cretaceous 70 80 90 100 110 120 130 140
Jurassic 150 160 170 180 190 200 210
Triassic 220 230 240

STEGOSAURUS

Stegosaurus, known for its large, sturdy build, was a herbivorous dinosaur that walked on all fours. It had a distinctive appearance, characterized by its rounded back, short front limbs, long hind limbs, and a tail held high in the air. One of the most recognizable features of Stegosaurus was its combination of broad, upright plates along its back and a tail tipped with spikes. The name Stegosaurus translates to 'roofed lizard' in Greek.

The purpose of these plates and spikes has been a topic of much discussion among scientists. Presently, it is widely believed that the spiked tail was primarily used for defense against predators, while the plates likely served as displays, possibly for attracting mates or intimidating rivals. Additionally, the plates might have played a role in regulating body temperature.

Stegosaurus had a relatively small brain compared to its body size. With its short neck and small head, it is thought to have fed on low-lying bushes and shrubs. Despite its imposing appearance, Stegosaurus was likely a peaceful herbivore, using its unique defensive adaptations only when necessary.

One thing is for sure, though, thanks in part to their distinctive combination of broad, upright, diamond-shaped plates and tail tipped with spikes, the Stegosaurus is one of the most recognizable dinosaurs ever!

1. In 1982, a well-known 'Far Side' comic by Gary Larson showed cavemen discussing a Stegosaurus tail with spikes, calling it the 'thagomizer,' named after a fictional caveman named Thag Simmons. Paleontologists have adopted this term and used it ever since!
2. Stegosaurus ate small rocks called gastroliths to help grind up tough plants in their massive stomach. To sustain its cold-blooded metab lism, it likely needed to devour hundreds of pounds of ferns and cycads every day.
3. The bony plates along the Stegosaurus's back were embedded in its skin and not connected to its skeleton.

Stegosaurus Stats

Period: Late Jurassic
Average Height: 9-14 feet
Average Length: 20 feet
Average Weight: 5 tons
Diet: Herbivore
Roamed: North America, Europe
Speed of about: 5-7 mph

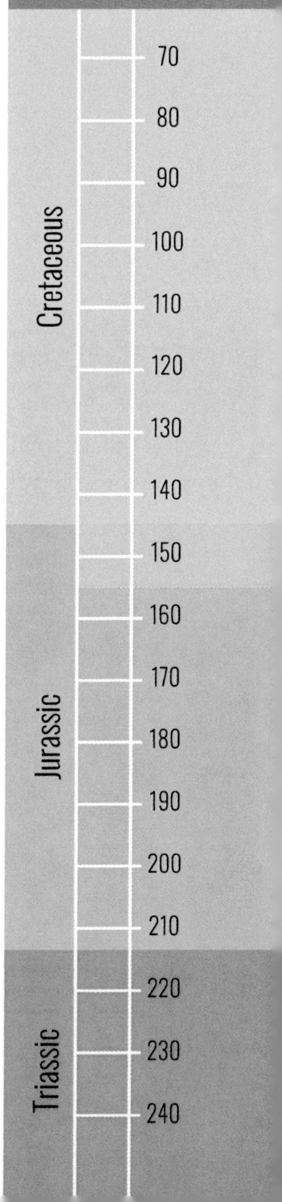

STEGOSAURUS

Cretaceous
Jurassic
Triassic

70
80
90
100
110
120
130
140
150
160
170
180
190
200
210
220
230
240

PTERANODON

The name Pteranodon translates to the words' winged and toothless,' a fitting description of its flying anatomy. The wings of Pteranodon and other pterosaurs were primarily composed of a membrane of skin and muscle that extended from their elongated fourth fingers to their hind limbs.

Pteranodon was one of the biggest flying reptiles, with a wingspan as broad as 9 to 20 feet! Even though many Pteranodon fossils are squished, we've found enough to know a lot about them.

Unlike their earlier flying cousins like Rhamphorhynchus and Pterodactylus, Pteranodon didn't have any teeth. Instead, they had beaks that looked a lot like those of birds we see today. These beaks were hard and bony, sticking out from their mouths. They were long, thin, and ended in sharp tips. The top part of the beak was longer than the bottom part.

The standout feature of Pteranodon is its main cranial crest. These crests were made of skull bones called frontals that jutted upward and backward from the head. The size and style of these crests could change because of different things like how old the Pteranodon was if it was a boy or a girl, and what species it belonged to.

Fun Facts about the Velociraptor

1. Pteranodon, arguably the most iconic of all pterosaurs, was once considered the largest flying animal ever! However, it was eventually surpassed in size by giant azhdarchids and the massive ornithocheirid Tropeognathus.
2. Due to the shape and structure of its wings, the Pteranodon most likely flew similarly to a modern-day albatross.
3. While a Pteradndon was a carnivore, it's generally classified as a piscivore, which means it primarily fed on fish.

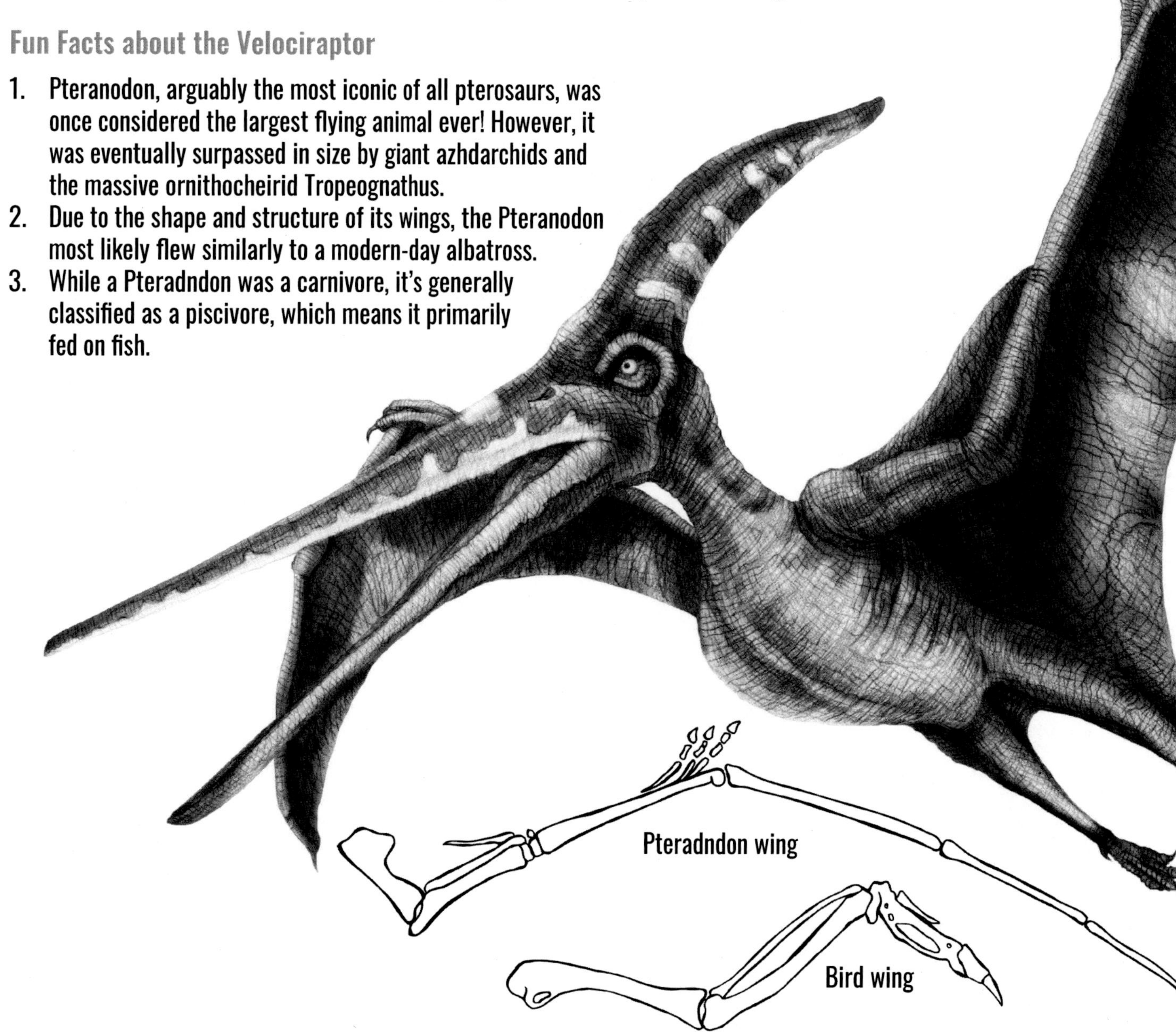

Pteranodon Stats

Period: Late Cretaceous
Average Height: 1.5-2 feet
Average Length: 16-33 feet
Average Weight: 50-100 pounds
Diet: Carnivore (Piscivore)
Roamed: North America
Speed of about: 30-40 mph

PTERANODON

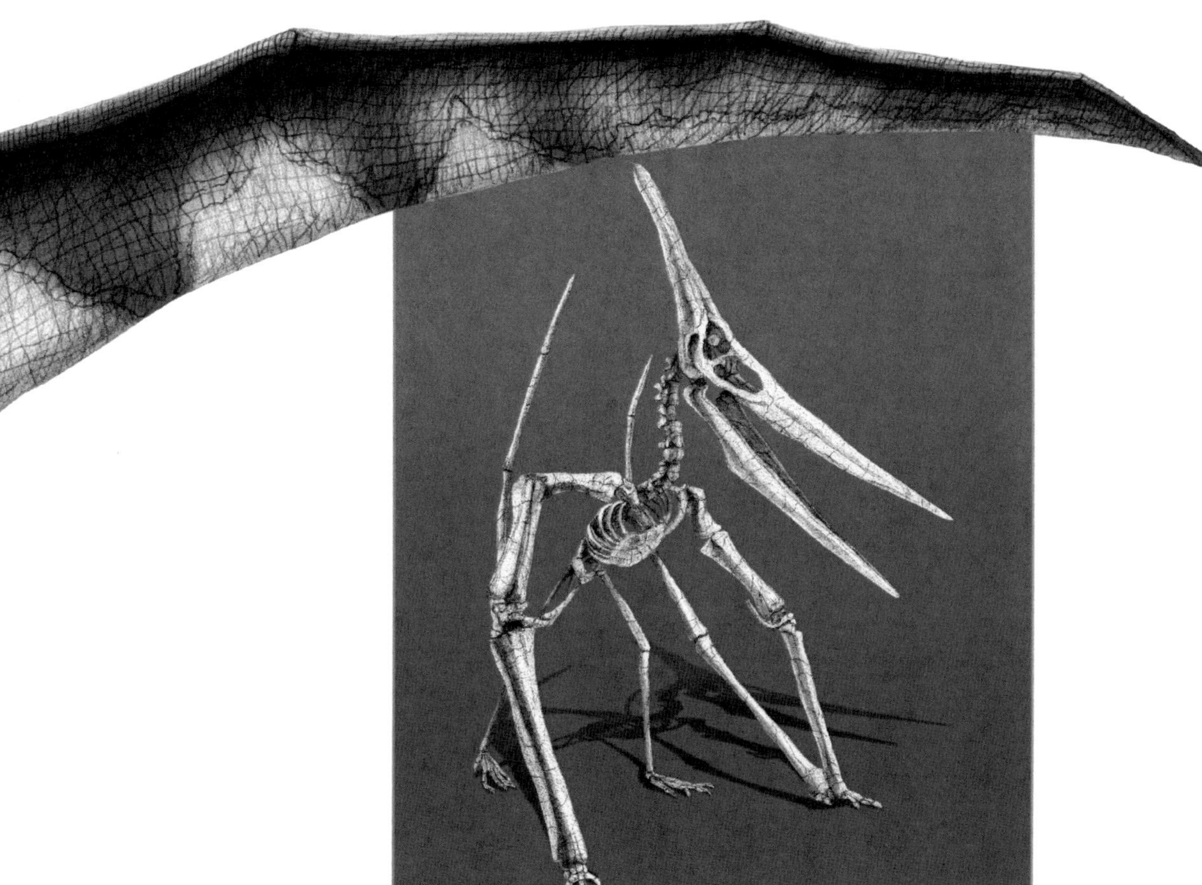

Cretaceous
Jurassic
Triassic

70
80
90
100
110
120
130
140
150
160
170
180
190
200
210
220
230
240

GALLIMIMUS

The Gallimimus belongs to a group of dinosaurs called ornithomimids, which were specially adapted lightweight theropods that became quite common toward the end of the Cretaceous period. Among these, Gallimimus stood out as one of the largest, possibly reaching lengths of six meters, though some fossil evidence suggests it could have been even larger, up to eight meters long!

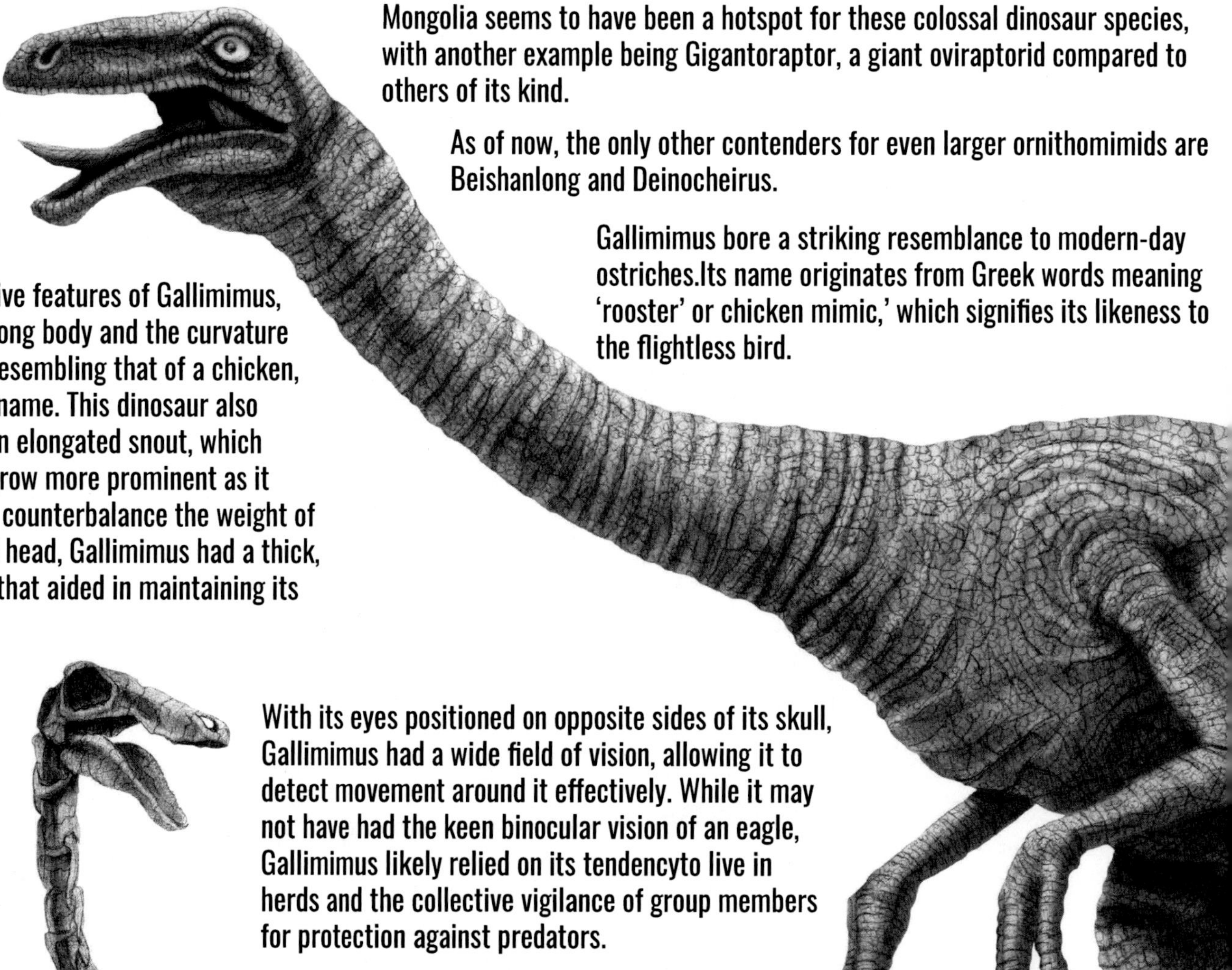

Mongolia seems to have been a hotspot for these colossal dinosaur species, with another example being Gigantoraptor, a giant oviraptorid compared to others of its kind.

As of now, the only other contenders for even larger ornithomimids are Beishanlong and Deinocheirus.

Gallimimus bore a striking resemblance to modern-day ostriches.Its name originates from Greek words meaning 'rooster' or chicken mimic,' which signifies its likeness to the flightless bird.

The distinctive features of Gallimimus, such as its long body and the curvature of its neck resembling that of a chicken, inspired its name. This dinosaur also possessed an elongated snout, which seemed to grow more prominent as it matured. To counterbalance the weight of its body and head, Gallimimus had a thick, flexible tail that aided in maintaining its balance.

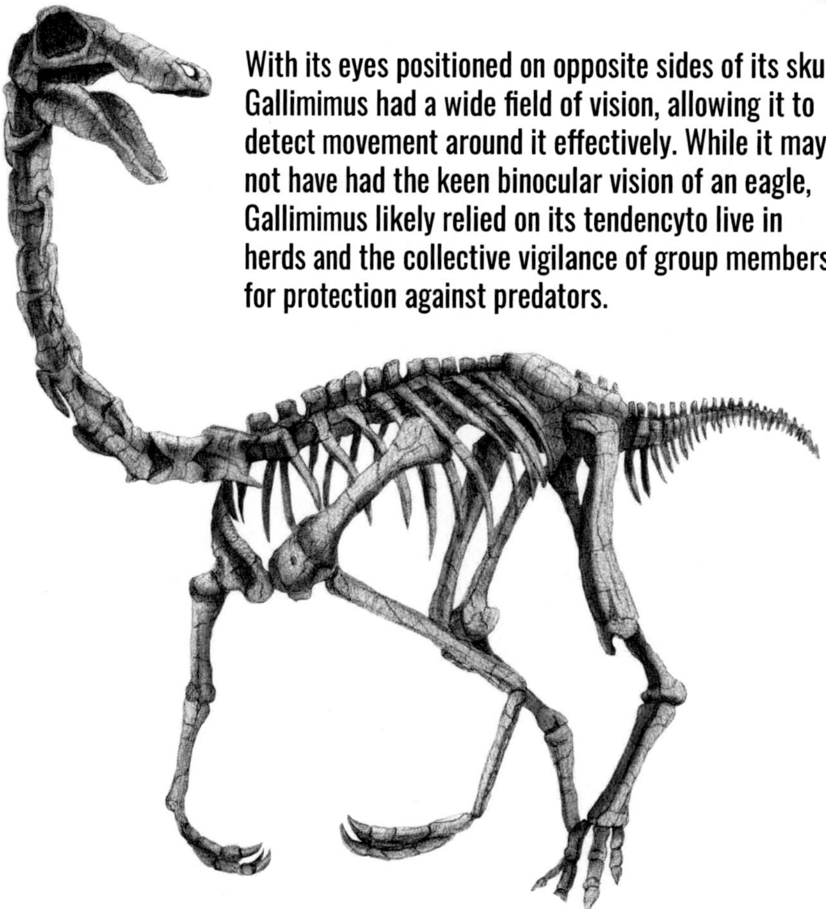

With its eyes positioned on opposite sides of its skull, Gallimimus had a wide field of vision, allowing it to detect movement around it effectively. While it may not have had the keen binocular vision of an eagle, Gallimimus likely relied on its tendencyto live in herds and the collective vigilance of group members for protection against predators.

GALLIMIMUS

Gallimimus Stats

Period: Late Cretaceous
Average Height: 6.5 feet
Average Length: 19-20 feet
Average Weight: 440-1100 pounds
Diet: Omnivore
Roamed: Mongolia
Speed of about: 40-50 mph

Fun Facts about the Gallimimus

1. The speed of a Gallimimus was estimated to be around 43 mph, which is right around the average sprinting speed of an ostrich.
2. Gallimimus is believed to have had a varied diet, including small cretaceous animals, insects, eggs, and plants. Its three claw-like fingers may have aided in digging into the soil to search for insects and also helped in holding and handling food.
3. Despite the Gallimimus being relatively quick, it still weighed just under half a ton, even with hollow bones.

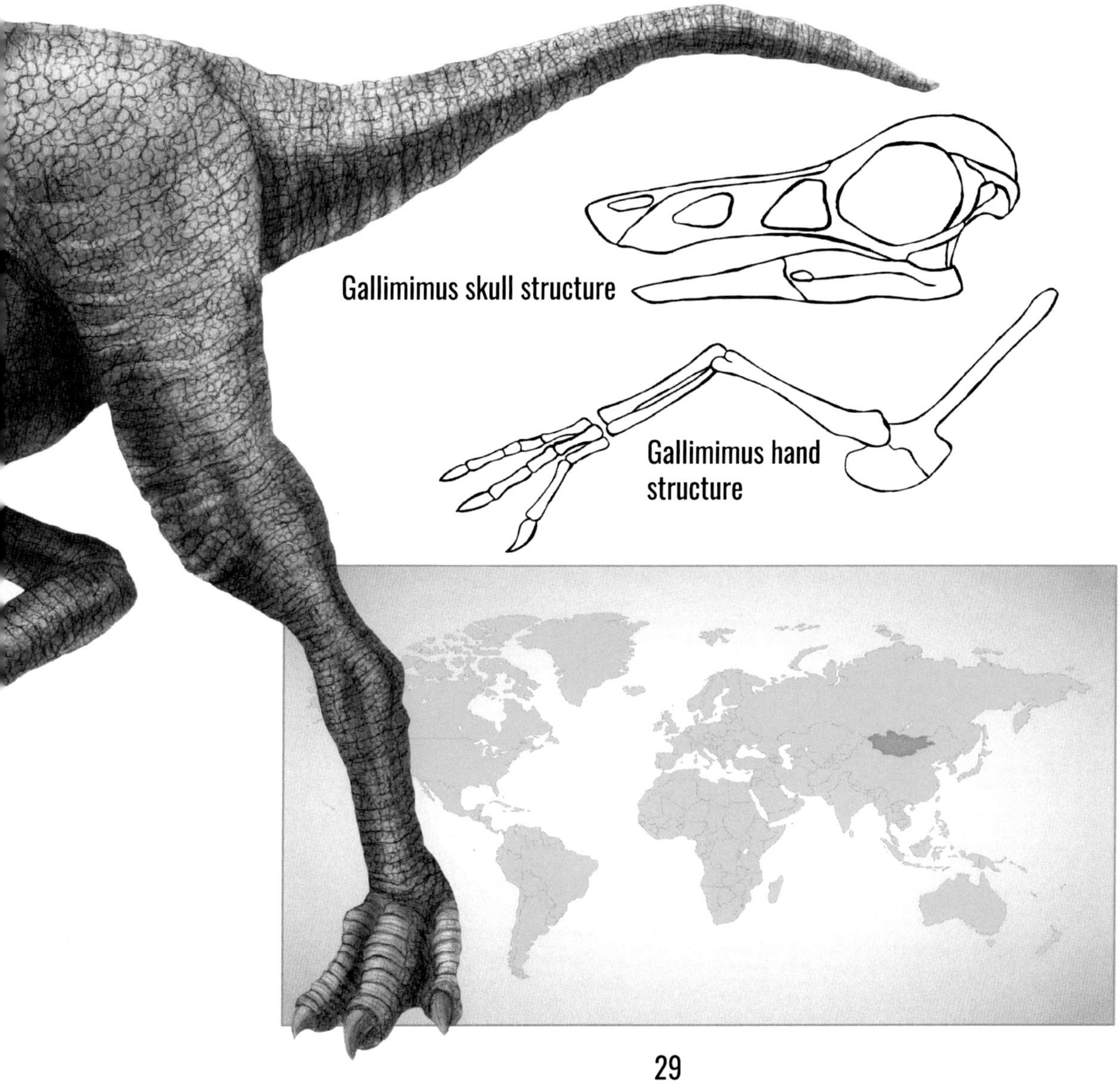

Gallimimus skull structure

Gallimimus hand structure

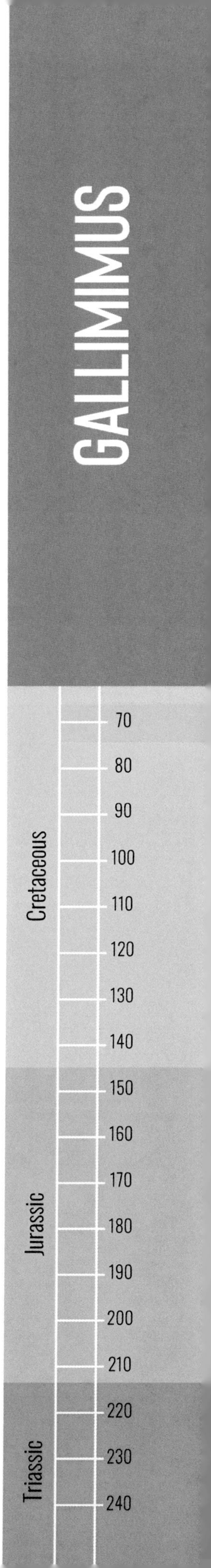

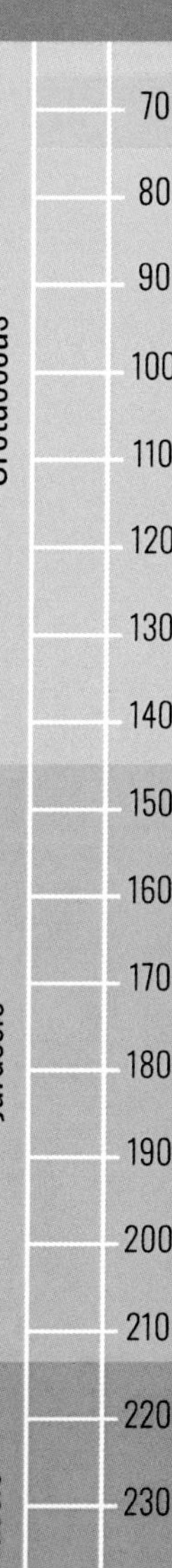

PARASAUROLOPHUS

The Parasaurolophus once roamed what is now North America during the Late Cretaceous Period. This unique creature had a long, distinctive head crest, which is where the meaning behind its name, 'lizard crest,' comes from. Fossil evidence tells us that Parasaurolophus had scaly skin, similar to modern reptiles.

Scientists have debated whether Parasaurolophus walked on two legs or four, but recent studies suggest it was a bit of both! It likely spent most of its time walking on all fours but could also stand up on its hind legs when needed.

Now, let's talk about that impressive crest! It was hollow and had a tube running through it, kind of like a big drinking straw. Scientists aren't entirely sure what it was used for, but they think it might have helped Parasaurolophus communicate with its pals through loud sounds or regulate its body temperature.

Have you ever wondered what it may be like to have a twin? Well, across the world, in China, there was a dinosaur called Charonosaurus that bore a striking resemblance to Parasaurolophus, which made some scientists believe they might be closely related or possibly the same species! As it would turn out later, the Charonosaurus was a whole different species altogether!

PARASAUROLOPHUS

Parasaurolophus Stats

Period: Late Cretaceous
Average Height: 8-10 feet
Average Length: 30-40 feet
Average Weight: 2.5-4 tons
Diet: Herbivore
Roamed: North America
Speed of about: 25-30 mph

Fun Facts about the Parasaurolophus

1. Not all Parasaurolophus had the same-sized crests. Some had smaller ones, which could indicate differences between males and females or even individuals of different ages.
2. Scientists have used computer models to recreate the sound Parasaurolophus might have made through its crest. It's a deep, trumpeting bellow that might have been used to warn others of danger. You can even listen to it online!
3. The mouth of the Parasaurolophus held more than 1,000 tiny teeth!

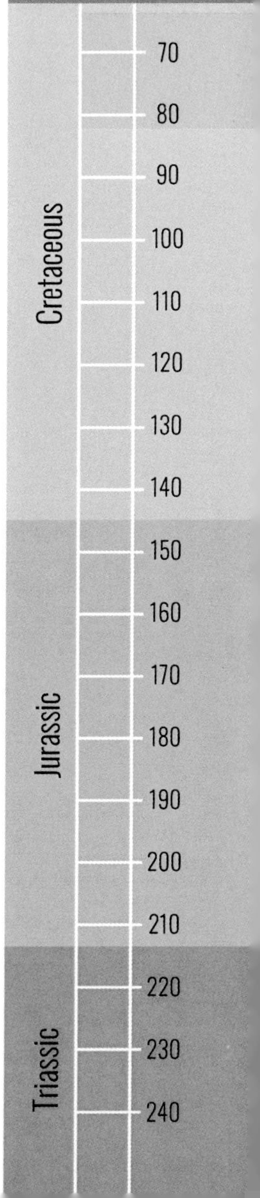

COMPSOGNATHUS

Compsognathus, also known as a Compy, was a tiny dinosaur that lived long ago in Germany and France. It was such a small dino that its name actually roughly means 'elegant,' 'refined,' or 'dainty.' It liked to hunt in packs and probably ate bugs and small lizards. We know this because the first fossil of Compsognathus had a lizard inside its stomach!

Some scientists argue about how many fingers Compsognathus had. Some say two, like a huge dinosaur called Tyrannosaurus. Others say three. Because we only have two fossils, and they're not perfectly preserved, it's hard to tell which side is right! We'd need to uncover some more specimens to be sure.

Compsognathus is also important because it helps us understand how birds evolved. It was found in the same place as Archaeopteryx, a reptile with feathers. They share lots of features, and other dinosaurs related to Compsognathus had feathers too. Scientists are eager to find more fossils to learn even more about this fascinating dinosaur.

Fun Facts about the Compsognathus

1. Many people used to think Compsognathus was as small as a chicken because of a German specimen. However, we now know that the fossil was likely a juvenile.
2. For decades, Compsognathus was thought to be the smallest known non-avian dinosaur, although some dinosaurs discovered later, such as Mahakala and Microraptor, were even smaller.
3. Compsognathus had a small head, just three inches long, while its tail was longer than its head, neck, and body combined.

Compsognathus Stats

Period: Late Jurassic
Average Height: 1 foot
Average Length: 3 feet
Average Weight: 2-3 lbs
Diet: Carnivore
Roamed: Europe
Speed of about: 25-30 mph

COMPSOGNATHUS

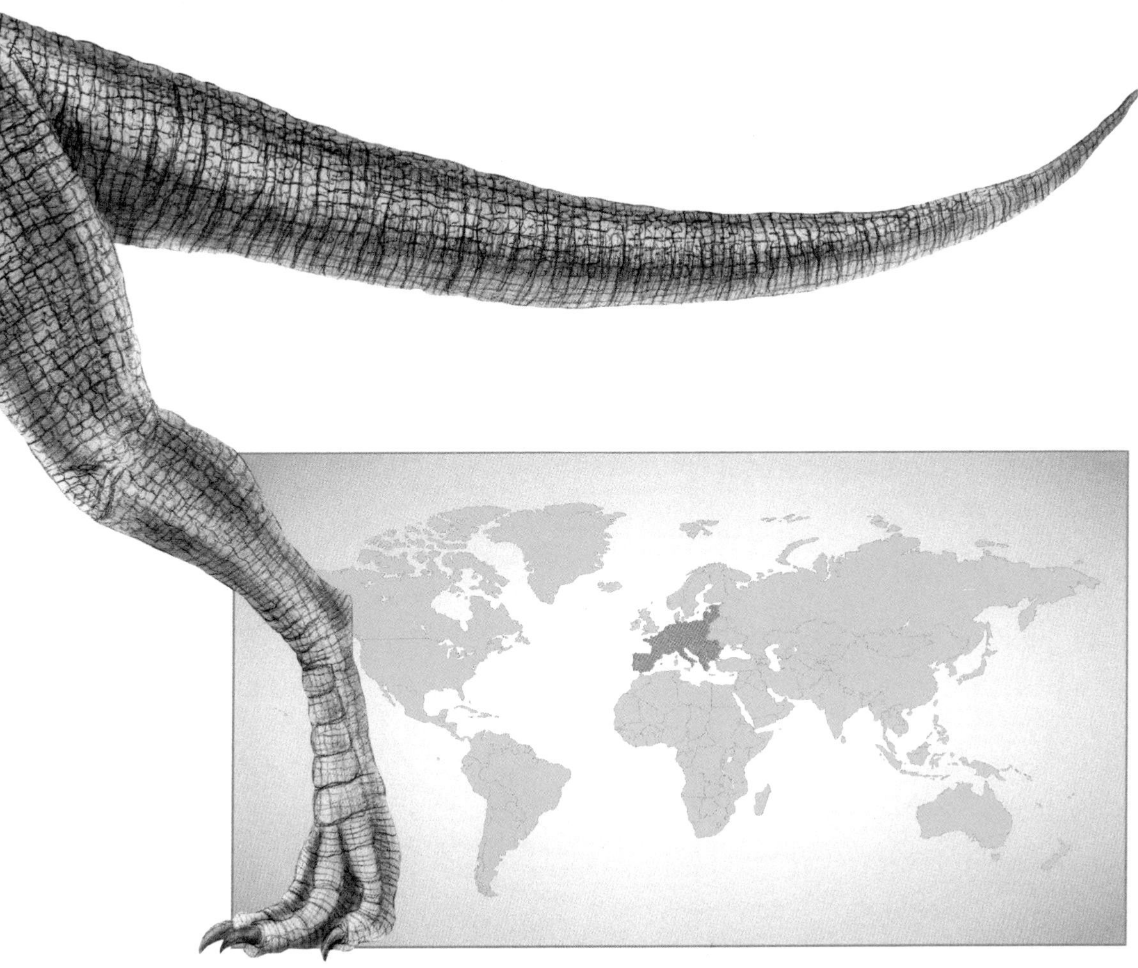

Cretaceous
Jurassic
Triassic

70
80
90
100
110
120
130
140
150
160
170
180
190
200
210
220
230
240

MAIASAURA

Maiasaura, which means 'good mother,' were big dinosaurs, reaching around 30 feet long and weighing about 4 tons. They had a wide mouth like a duck and lots of teeth, just like other dinosaurs in their family.

One thing that made Maiasaura special was the short, solid crest between their eyes. Some scientists think they used it to bump heads with each other during mating season. These dinosaurs only ate plants, and they could walk on two legs or four legs. When they were young, they walked mostly on two legs, but as they got older and bigger, they switched to four legs.

Maiasaura didn't have many weapons, but they could kick, stomp, or use their strong tails to defend themselves. They probably ran away from danger, especially since they lived in huge herds, sometimes with as many as 10,000 dinosaurs together. Scientists have found lots of Maiasaura fossils, from babies to adults, which helps them understand how these dinosaurs grew.

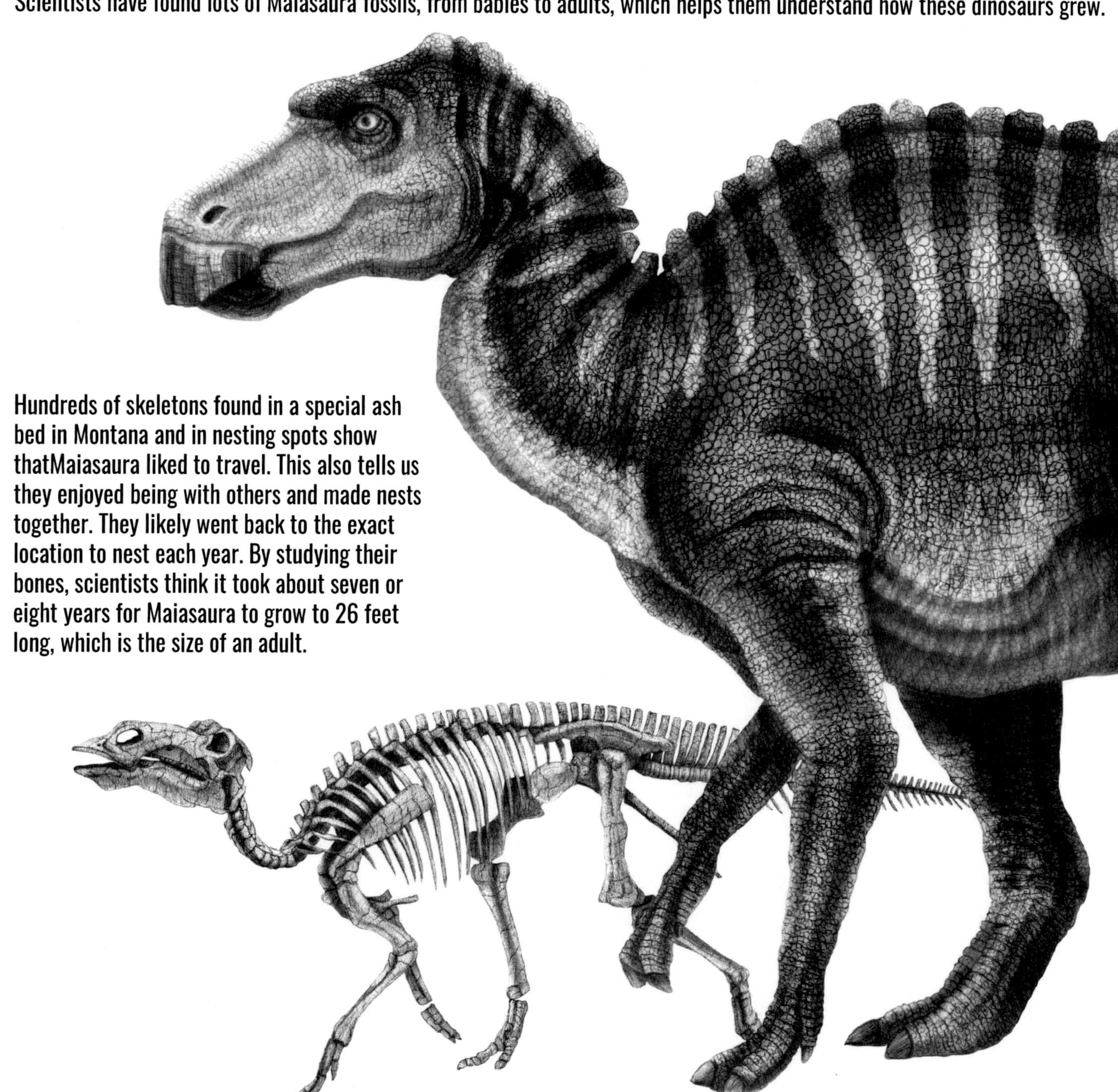

Hundreds of skeletons found in a special ash bed in Montana and in nesting spots show thatMaiasaura liked to travel. This also tells us they enjoyed being with others and made nests together. They likely went back to the exact location to nest each year. By studying their bones, scientists think it took about seven or eight years for Maiasaura to grow to 26 feet long, which is the size of an adult.

Maiasaura Stats

Period: Late Cretaceous
Average Height: 15 feet
Average Length: 25-35 feet
Average Weight: 3-4 tons
Diet: Herbivore
Roamed: North America
Speed of about: 25-30 mph

MAIASAURA

Fun Facts about the Maiasaura

1. Maiasaura is notable for being the first dinosaur found alongside its young, including a nest and eggs. This suggests that adult Maiasaura were nurturing and cared for their young.
2. When Maiasaura babies hatched, they couldn't walk or eat by themselves. So, the parents had to bring food and protect them from predators.
3. In the first year, the hatchlings experienced a rapid growth spurt from 16 to 58 inches Paleontologists believe this high growth rate could indicate that they were warm-blooded.

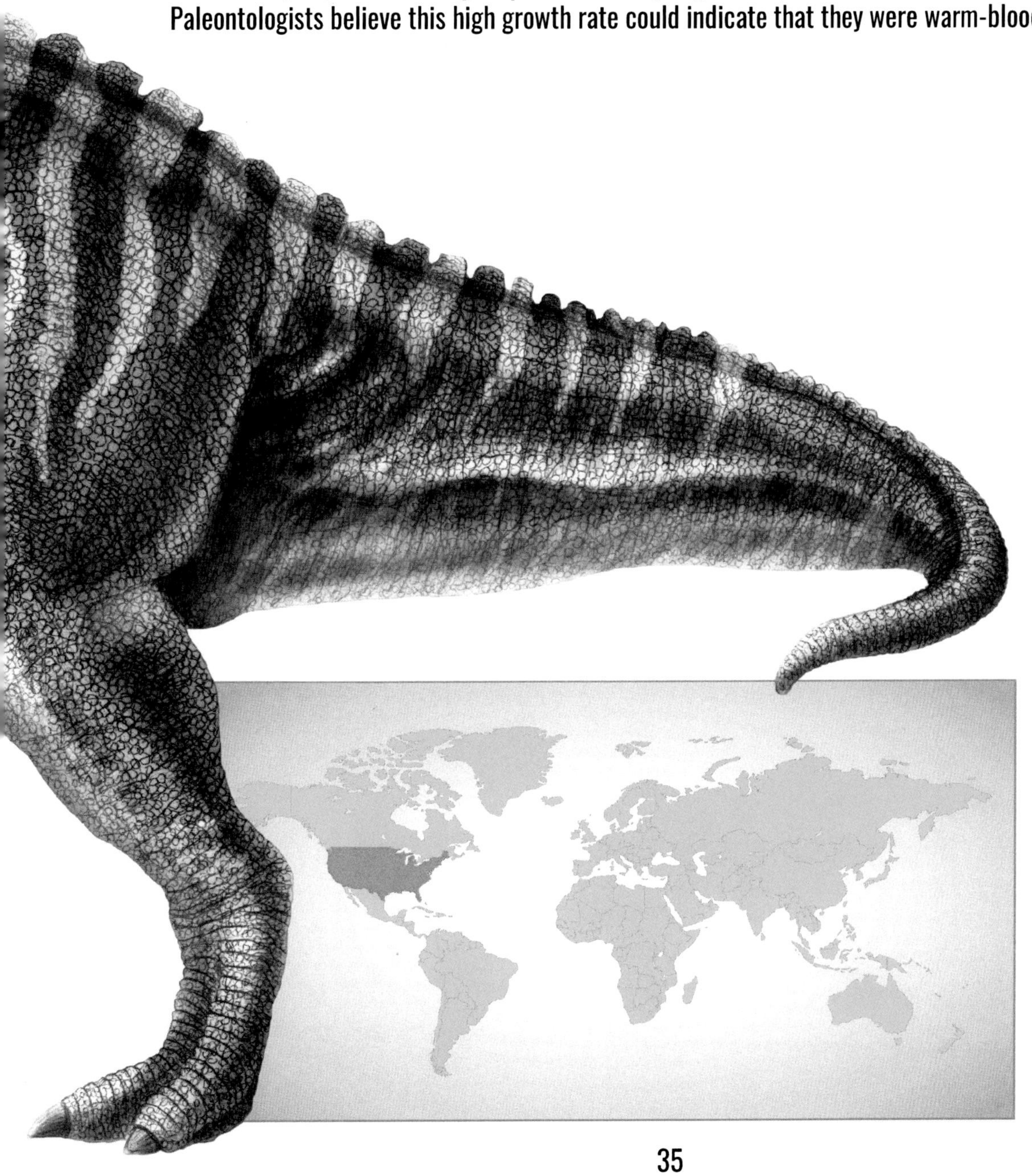

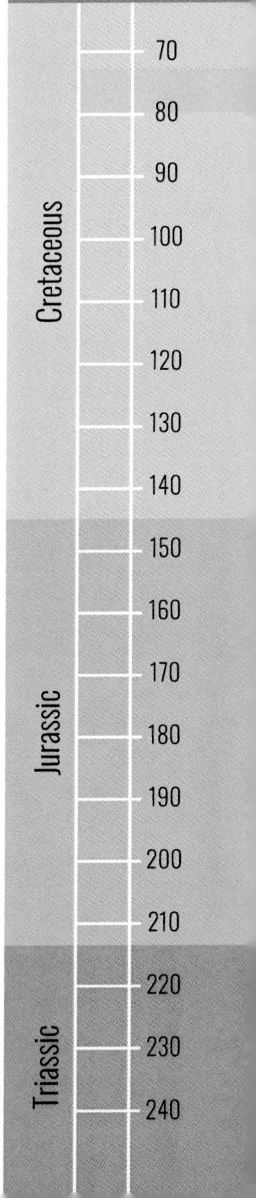

Cretaceous
Jurassic
Triassic
70 80 90 100 110 120 130 140 150 160 170 180 190 200 210 220 230 240

MOSASAURUS

Mosasaurus, whose name means 'lizard of the Meuse River,' in reference to where it was discovered, was one of the first Mesozoic marine reptiles known to science. These aquatic goliaths were like giant snakes of the sea.

They had giant skulls and long noses. Their arms and legs turned into paddles with shorter bones and more fingers and toes than their ancestors. Their tails were long and curved slightly, similar to early ichthyosaurs. They had over 100 vertebrae in their backbone.

Their skull looked a lot like modern monitor lizards, which are actually related to Mosasaurs. They had lots of sharp teeth in their jaws, and their jawbones could move in the middle, only connected at the front by ligaments. This helped them open their mouths wide and move their jaws sideways to eat big prey.

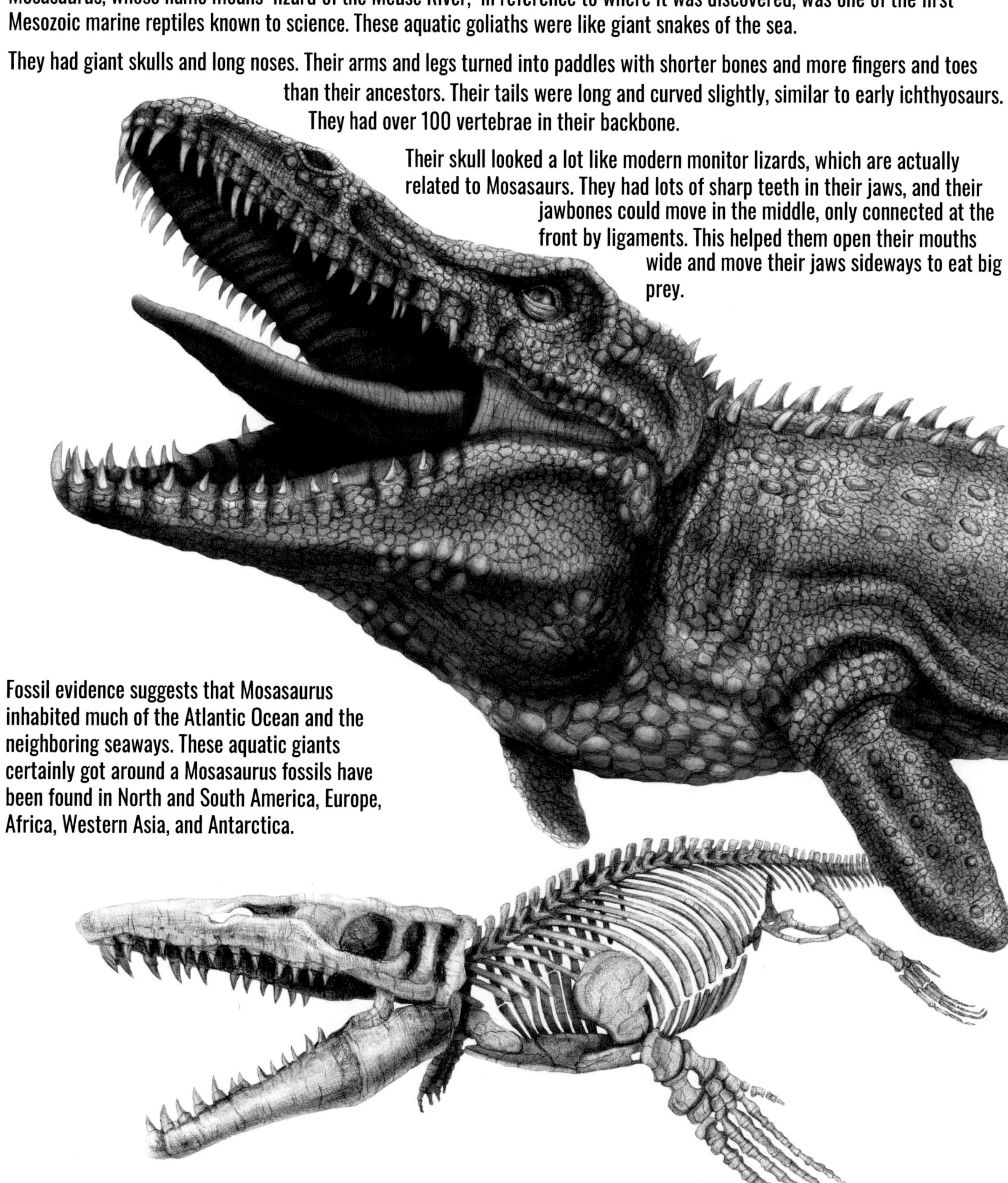

Fossil evidence suggests that Mosasaurus inhabited much of the Atlantic Ocean and the neighboring seaways. These aquatic giants certainly got around a Mosasaurus fossils have been found in North and South America, Europe, Africa, Western Asia, and Antarctica.

Mosasaurus Stats

Period: Late Cretaceous
Average Length: 40-50 feet
Average Weight: 15-25 tons
Diet: Carnivore (Piscivore)
Roamed: Global distribution, primarily in shallow seas)
Speed of about: 30 mph

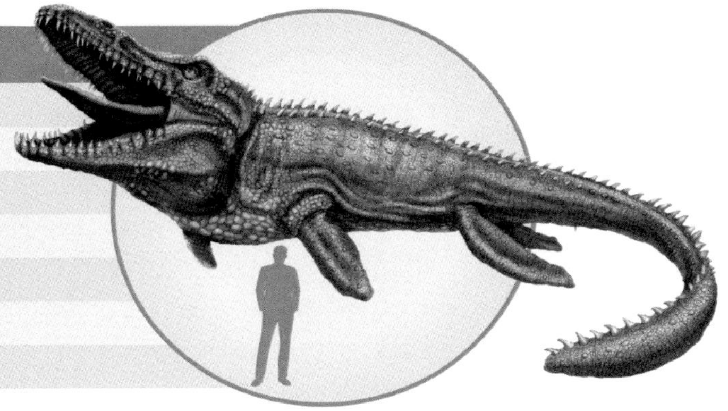

Fun Facts about the Mosasaurus

1. Over 30 different specimens of Mosasaurus have been discovered by paleontologists.
2. Mosasaurus had around 40-50 massive teeth, which were conical and sharp and allowed them to swallow their prey whole, much like modern snakes.
3. Early paleontologists thought that the Mosasaur might be an ancient crocodile or monitor lizard. However, later, they realized it was a distinct species unrelated to any modern animal.

One of the food items of mosasaurs were ammonites, molluscs with shells similar to those of Nautilus, which were abundant in the Cretaceous seas. Holes have been found in fossil shells of some ammonites, mainly Pachydiscus and Placenticeras.

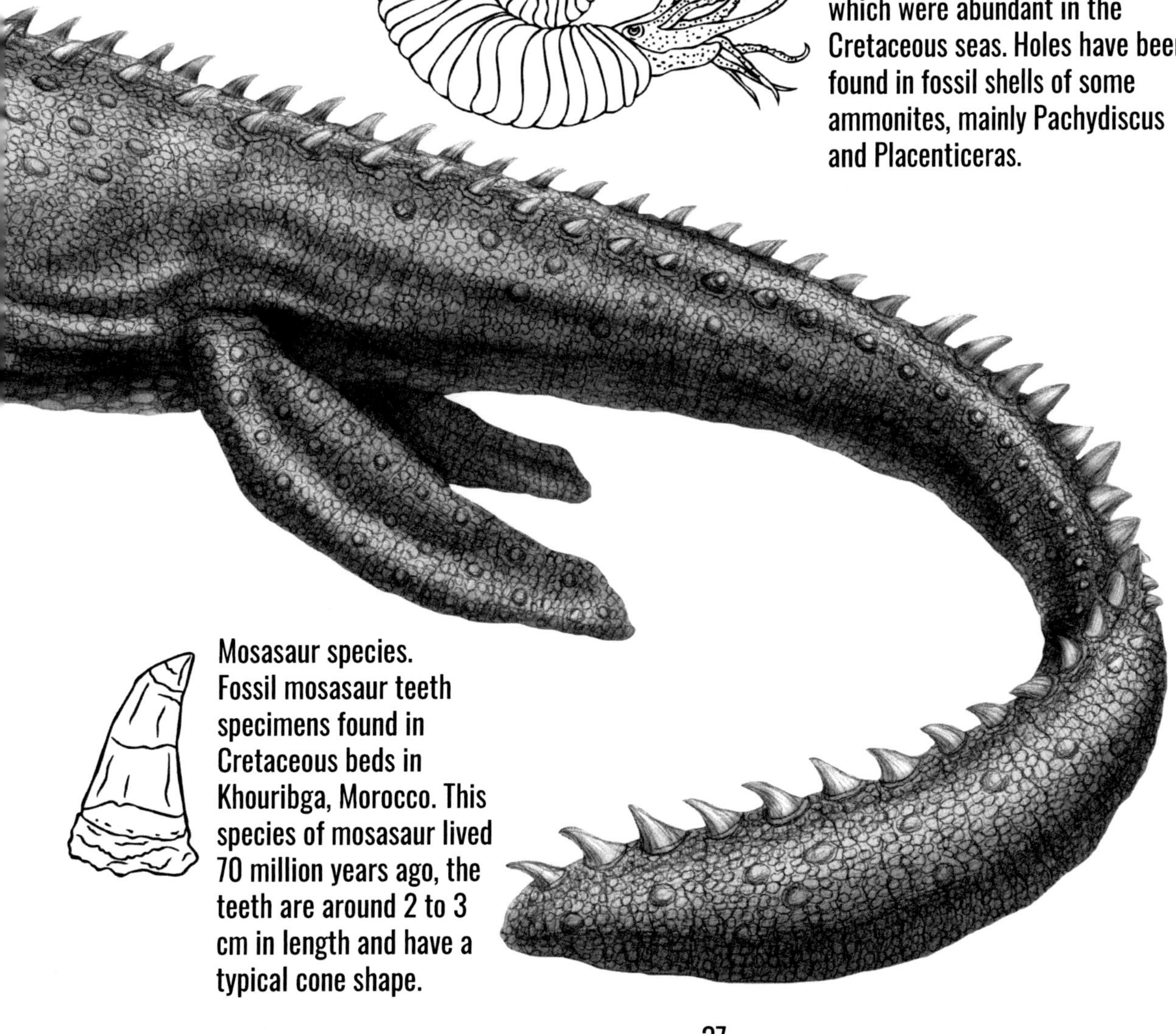

Mosasaur species. Fossil mosasaur teeth specimens found in Cretaceous beds in Khouribga, Morocco. This species of mosasaur lived 70 million years ago, the teeth are around 2 to 3 cm in length and have a typical cone shape.

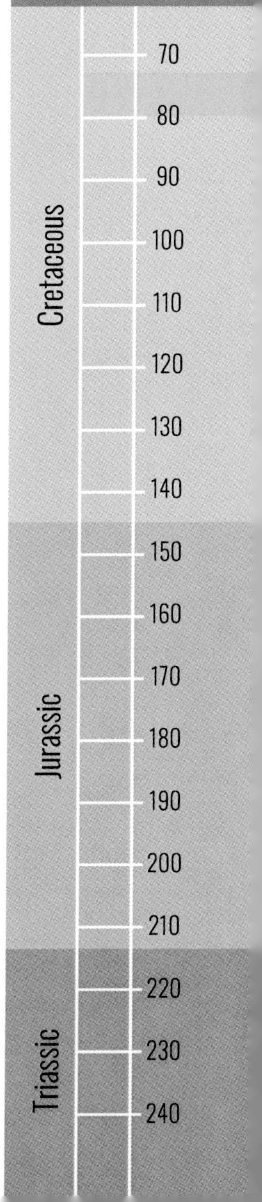

Cretaceous: 70, 80, 90, 100, 110, 120, 130, 140
Jurassic: 150, 160, 170, 180, 190, 200, 210
Triassic: 220, 230, 240

STYGIMOLOCH

Stygimoloch, meaning 'demon from the river Styx,' is a genus within the pachycephalosaur family that lived during the Late Cretaceous period. It stood out from other pachycephalosaurs because of the row of spikes on the back of its head, located behind the characteristic dome of the family.

Stygimoloch enjoyed a plant-based diet and walked on two legs, thriving during the late Cretaceous period, around 70 to 66 million years ago.

It had a very thick skull and long hind legs but short arms. Stygimoloch probably used its head to butt others in defense or when fighting with each other.

Researchers found that 22% of all Stygimoloch skulls they studied had signs of infection, likely from injuries. This suggests that these dinosaurs might have used their thick skulls to fight with each other.

Stygimoloch Stats

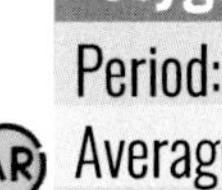

Period: Late Cretaceous
Average Height: 5-6 feet
Average Length: 7-12 feet
Average Weight: 200 lbs
Diet: Herbivore
Roamed: North America
Speed of about: 20-30 mph

Most likely, the horns and spikes of Stygimoloch were used for jousting, mainly through head-butting and flank-butting. It's also believed that the horns also served as ornamentation, potentially aiding in identification and mating.

The first fossils of Stygimoloch were found in North America, in Montana and Wisconsin. The first one was discovered in Hell Creek, Montana, and was named in 1983.

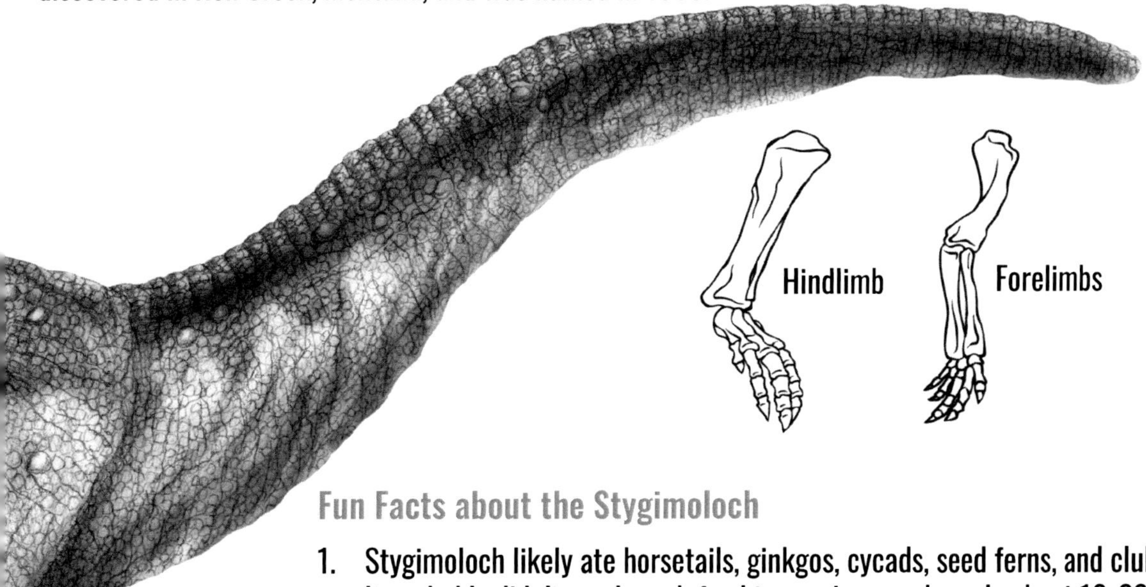

Hindlimb

Forelimbs

Fun Facts about the Stygimoloch

1. Stygimoloch likely ate horsetails, ginkgos, cycads, seed ferns, and club mosses. It probably didn't need much food to survive, maybe only about 10-20 pounds of vegetation a day.
2. Stygimoloch has 5 fingers on its forelimbs but only 3 toes on each hindlimb.
3. 22% of all examined pachycephalosaurid domes showed lesions indicating osteomyelitis, a bone infection often caused by trauma. This suggests that these domes were likely used in combat between members of the same species.

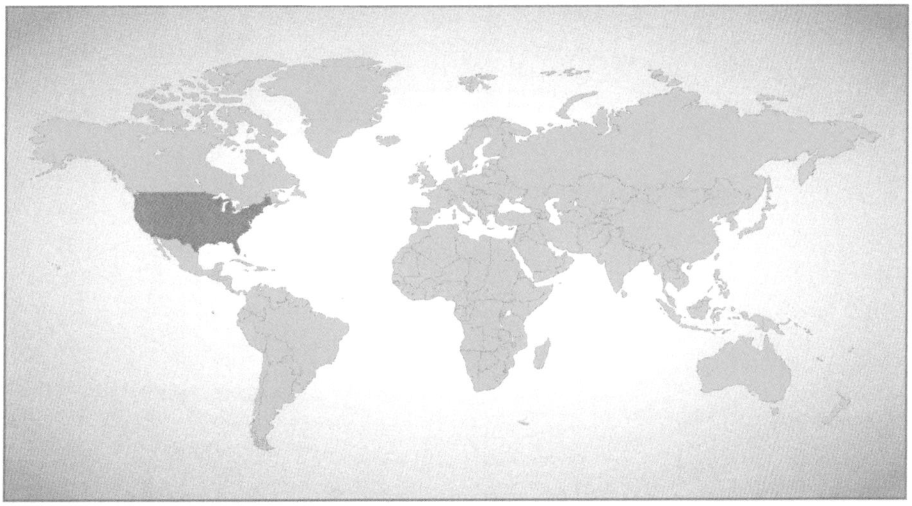

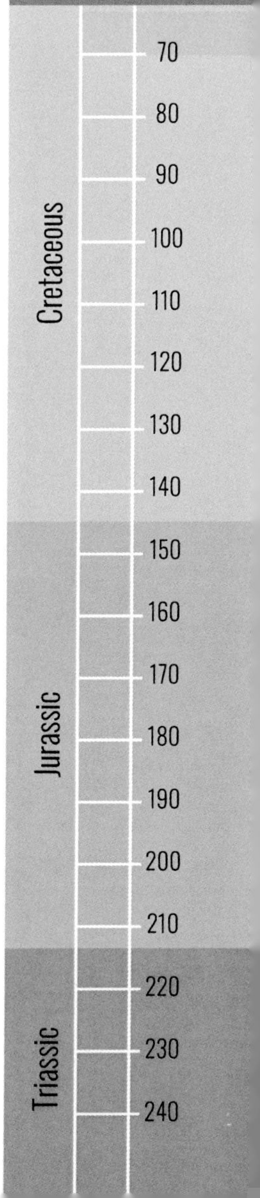

CARNOTAURUS

The name Carnotaurus comes from the Latin words "carno," meaning "flesh," and "taurus," meaning "bull," translating to "meat-eating bull," which refers to the dinosaur's bull-like horns. Carnotaurus was a special kind of dinosaur called a theropod. What made it special? Well, it had thick horns above its eyes, something you didn't see in other meat-eating dinosaurs. Its skull was deep and sat on a strong neck. And its arms were so tiny, even smaller than those of a Tyrannosaurus!

When scientists found its remains, they saw imprints of its skin. It had lots of small scales, like a pattern on a picture. There were also big bumps on its sides. But there were no signs of feathers.

Carnotaurus might have used its horns and strong neck to fight with other Carnotaurus dinosaurs. They might have banged their heads together or pushed each other slowly. They might have even run into each other, using their horns like bumpers!

Scientists aren't sure precisely what Carnotaurus ate. Some think it could hunt big dinosaurs like sauropods, while others believe it mostly ate smaller animals. But one thing's for sure: Carnotaurus was built for speed. It might have been one of the fastest big, meat-eating dinosaurs ever to roam the Earth!

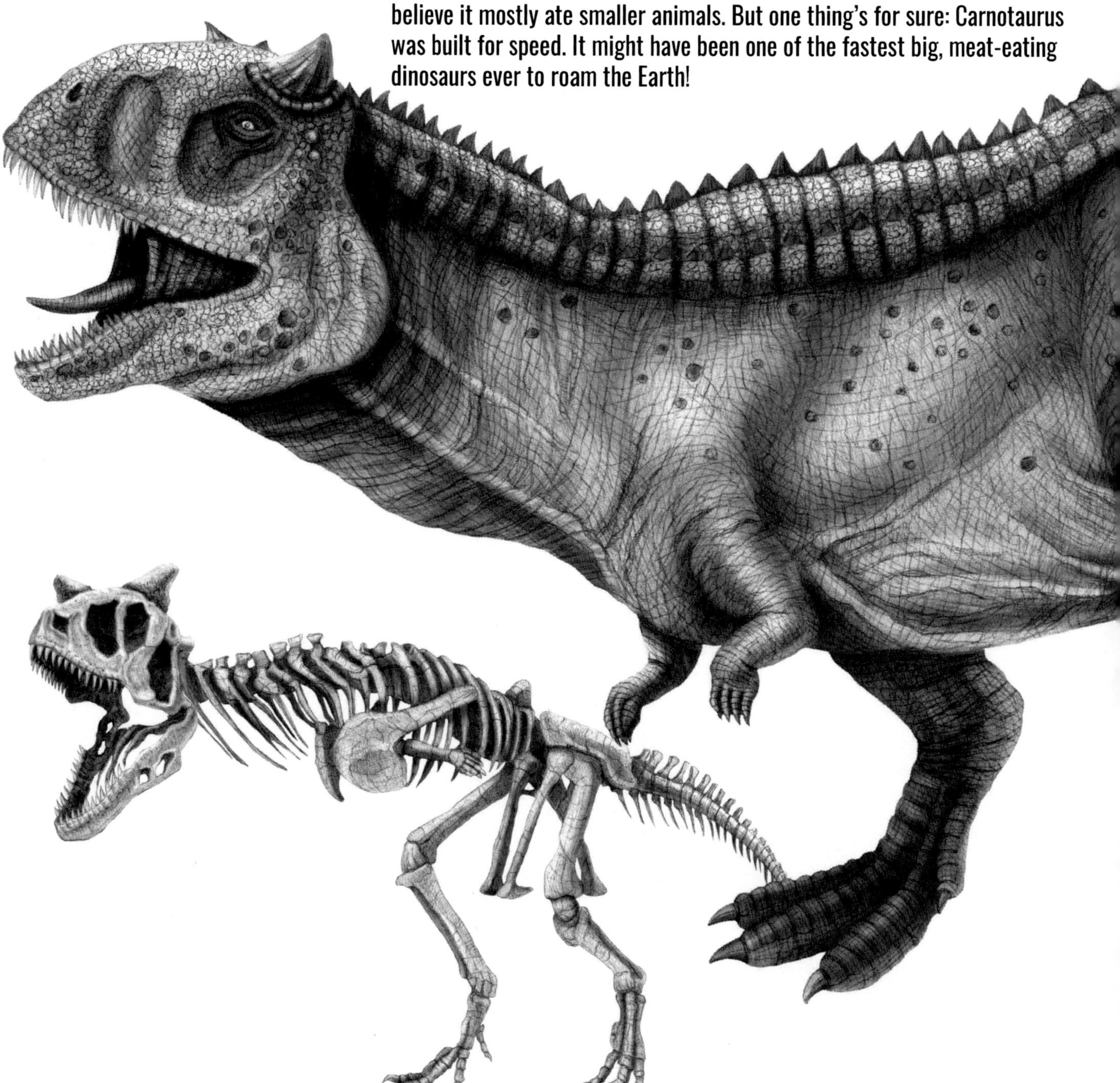

Carnotaurus Stats

Period: Late Cretaceous
Average Height: 9-10 feet
Average Length: 25-30 feet
Average Weight: 1-2 tons
Diet: Carnivore
Roamed: South America (Argentina)
Speed of about: 30-35 mph

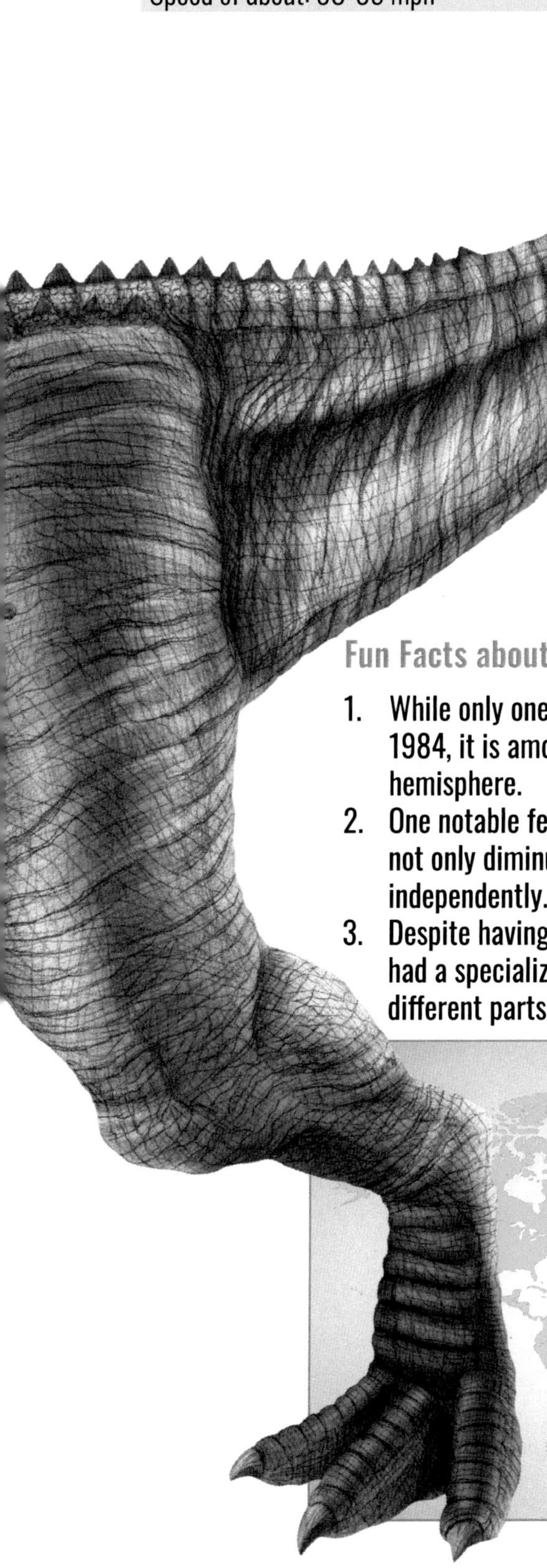

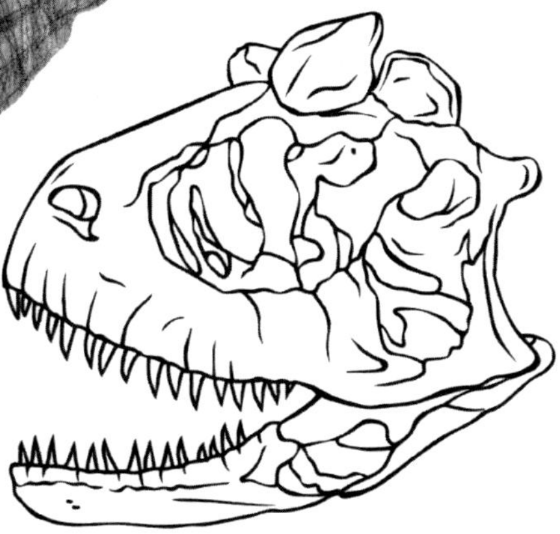

CARNOTAURUS

Fun Facts about the Carnotaurus

1. While only one well-preserved skeleton exists, which was discovered in 1984, it is among the most thoroughly studied theropods from the southern hemisphere.
2. One notable feature of this dinosaur is its extremely small arms, which are not only diminutive but also have fused fingers, restricting them from moving independently.
3. Despite having a weaker bite force than other large theropods, Carnotaurus had a specialized skull that was flexible, called a kinetic skull. This allowed different parts of the skull to move while eating, reducing stress on the bone.

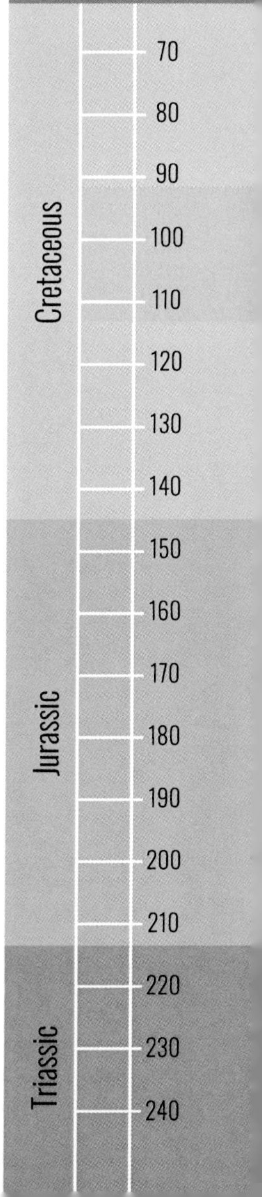

ALLOSAURUS

Allosaurus, which translates to means "different lizard," was a big predator that walked on two legs. Its skull was strong and had lots of sharp, saw-like teeth. It was about 28 feet long on average, but some were even longer, up to 32 feet! Its legs were powerful, and it had three small fingers on each hand. Since they were so large, their bodies had to be balanced by their long tail.

This dinosaur was one of the top hunters of its time. It liked to eat other big dinosaurs, like plant-eaters such as ornithopods, stegosaurids, and sauropods. Sometimes, it might even hunt other predators!

Some scientists think Allosaurus hunted in groups, working together to catch their food. But others believe they were more like loners, fighting over meals when they found them. Either way, Allosaurus was a mighty hunter of its time!

ALLOSAURUS

Allosaurus Stats

Period: Late Jurassic
Average Height: 12-17 feet
Average Length: 28-40 feet
Average Weight: 2-3 tons
Diet: Carnivore
Roamed: North America, Europe, Africa
Speed of about: 19-34 mph

Fun Facts about the Allosaurus

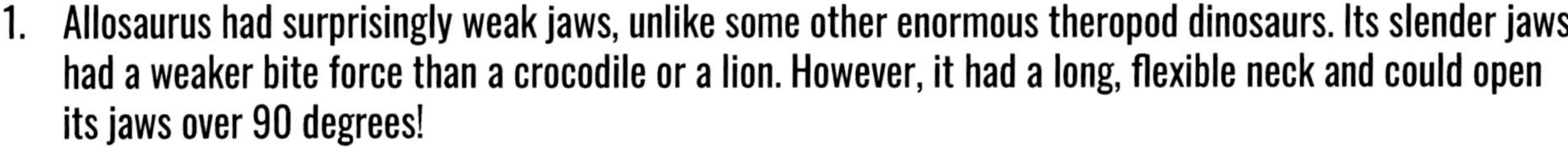

1. Allosaurus had surprisingly weak jaws, unlike some other enormous theropod dinosaurs. Its slender jaws had a weaker bite force than a crocodile or a lion. However, it had a long, flexible neck and could open its jaws over 90 degrees!
2. Allosaurus continuously grew, shed, and replaced its teeth, with some reaching three to four inches in length. Despite this, it only had about 32 teeth, with 16 in each upper and lower jaw at any given time.
3. Most people believe the T-Rex to be the biggest movie star of all the dinos, and while this may be true, the Allosaurus actually appeared on the big screen first!It starred as a prehistoric protagonist in the 1925 movie The Lost World.

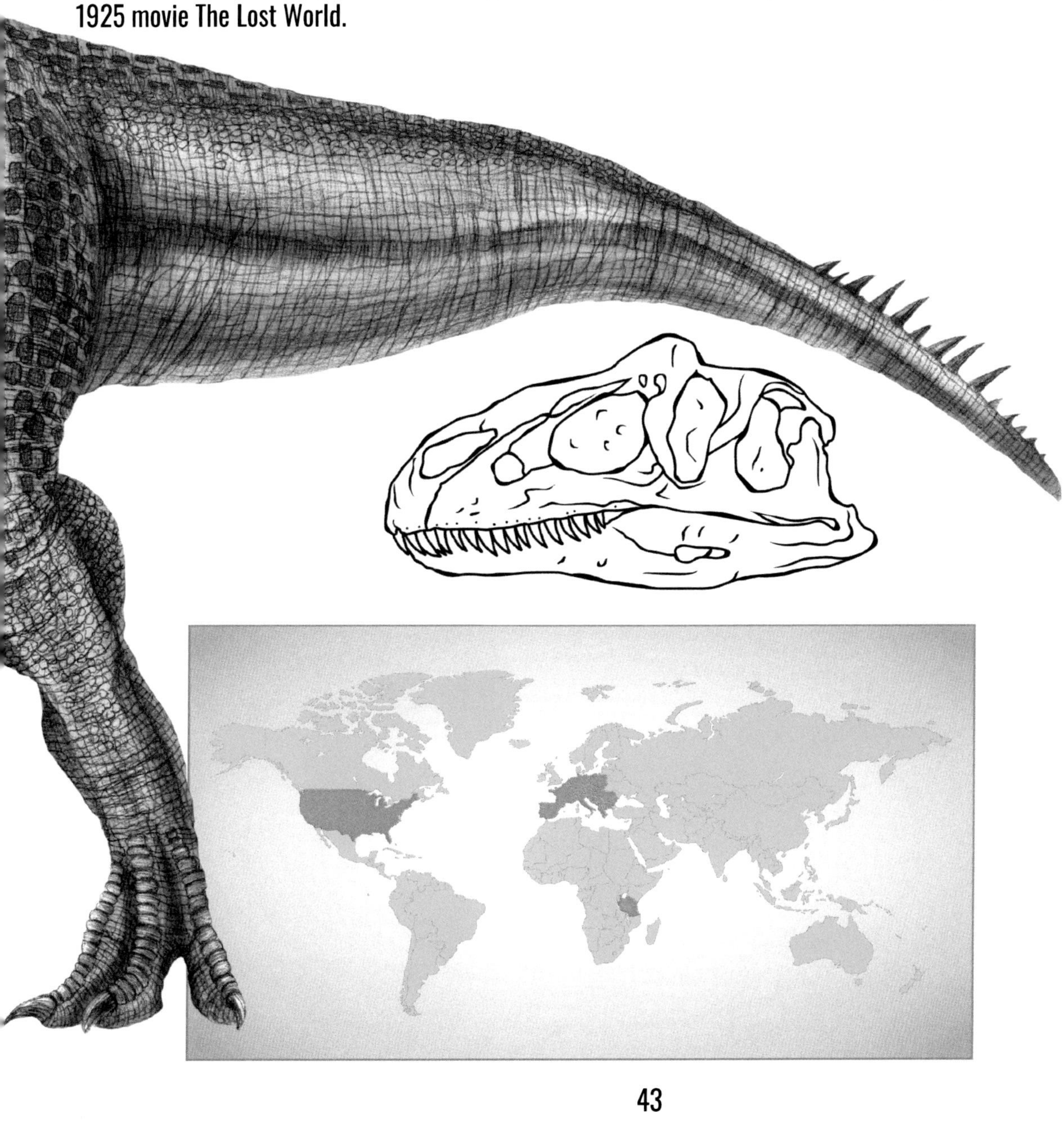

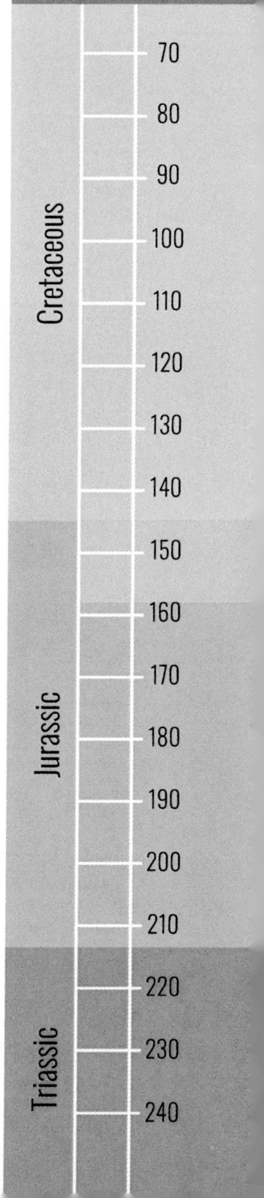

ANKYLOSAURUS

Ankylosaurus, which translates to "fused lizard," was a huge dinosaur, possibly one of the biggest of its kind. On average, they're believed to be around 26 feet long and weigh around 8 tons. This dinosaur walked on all fours with a strong, sturdy body.

Its head was wide and low, with two horns pointing backward from the back of its skull and two more horns below them, pointing backward and down. Unlike other dinosaurs like it, its nostrils faced sideways instead of forward. Its front jaws had a beak with rows of small, leaf-shaped teeth behind it. Ankylosaurus was covered in armor plates called osteoderms, with bony half-rings around its neck. And the most famous feature? A big club on the end of its tail!

It probably wasn't speedy, but it could move quickly when it needed to. It liked to eat lots of different plants, and scientists think the strange chambers in its snout might have helped it stay cool or make sounds. That tail club wasn't just for show. It was probably used to defend against predators or to fight with other Ankylosaurus dinosaurs. With its tough armor and powerful tail, Ankylosaurus was a force to be reckoned with!

Fun Facts about the Ankylosaurus

1. While slow, this dino was not an easy target for big carnivores. With a quick whack of its clubbed tail, Ankylosaurus could likely shatter a T-Rex's bones, perhaps even killing it in the process.
2. The famous dinosaur hunter Barnum Brown, also known as Mr. Bones, is credited with the first discovery of an Ankylosaurus fossil in 1906.
3. Studies of the Ankylosaurus skull suggest that they had an extraordinary sense of smell, which means they could most likely catch the scent of a predator from a reasonable distance.

Ankylosaurus Stats

Period: Late Cretaceous
Average Height: 5-6 feet
Average Length: 20-35 feet
Average Weight: 4-9 tons
Diet: Herbivore
Roamed: North America
Speed of about: 5-7 mph

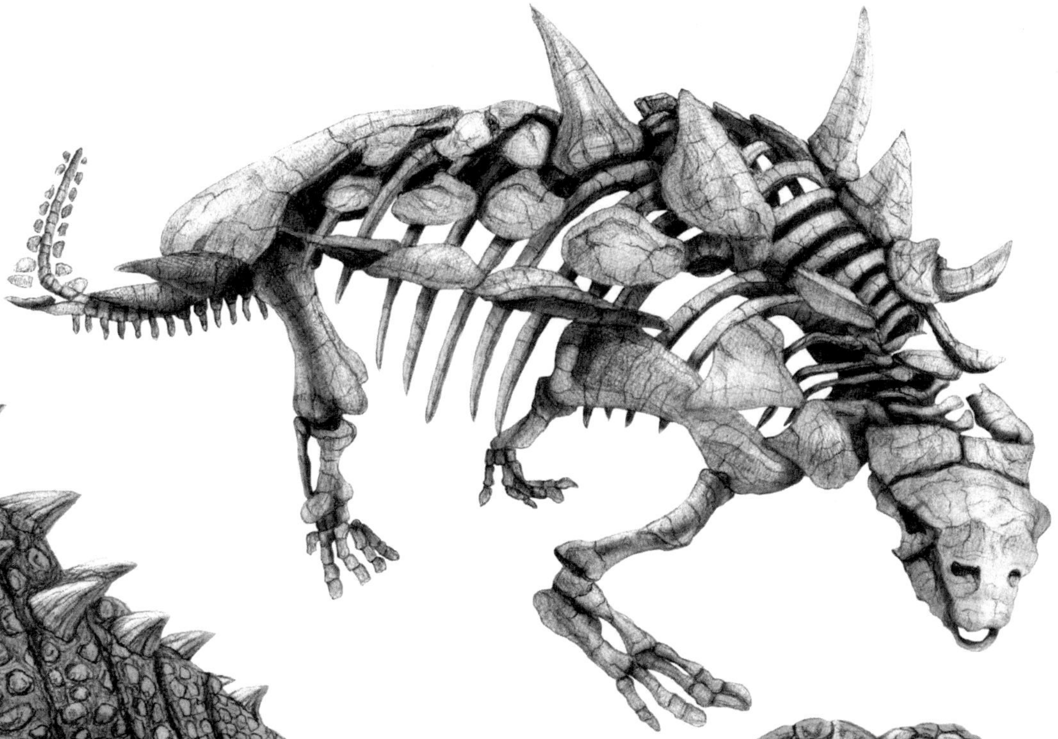

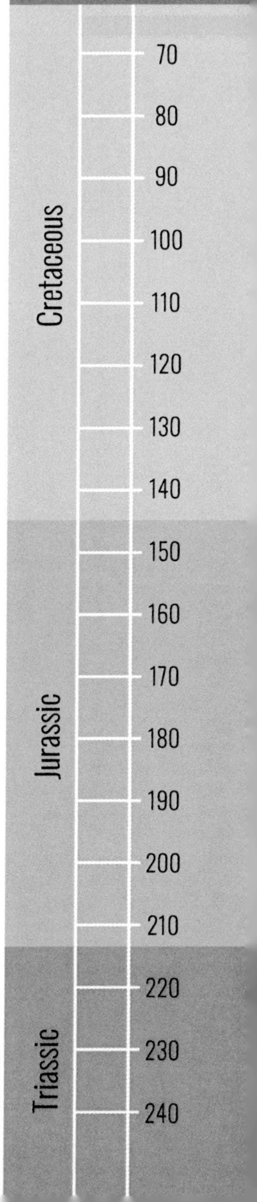

ANKYLOSAURUS

Cretaceous
Jurassic
Triassic

70
80
90
100
110
120
130
140
150
160
170
180
190
200
210
220
230
240

ARGENTINOSAURUS

Argentinosaurus, which translates to "Argentine lizard," was a massive sauropod dinosaur that roamed Argentina during the Late Cretaceous period. It's known for being one of the largest land animals ever discovered, even though we only have bits and pieces of its skeleton. Scientists use the bones we do have to compare with other, more complete sauropod skeletons to guess how big Argentinosaurus might have been.

Because of its enormous size, Argentinosaurus belongs to a group of sauropods called titanosaurs. These giants were lightly armored and could be found all over the world during the later part of the Cretaceous period.

Argentinosaurus's closest relative among titanosaurs seems to be Saltasaurus, a much smaller dinosaur weighing in at only 10 tons. Saltasaurus lived a few million years after Argentinosaurus.

The Argentinosaurus laid eggs. Despite their enormous size, the eggs were about the size of a beach ball. They were probably no longer than 3.3 feet (1 meter) and weighed about 11 pounds (5 kilograms).

Fun Facts about the Argentinosaurus

1. Argentinosaurus eggs are estimated to have been around a foot in diameter, and females laid up to 10 or 15 eggs at once. This increased the chances that at least one hatchling would escape predators and grow into an adult.
2. Considering the enormous size of Argentinosaurus, it's possible that a newborn hatchling took three or four decades to reach full size, which means it would undergo approximately a 25,000 percent increase in bulk from hatchling to adult.
3. Scientists aren't sure if Argentinosaurus held its neck up high to eat leaves from tall trees or if it kept it lower while eating. This is a mystery for many long-necked dinosaurs like Argentinosaurus. One reason is that holding its neck high would have made its heart work really hard, pumping blood up so high (around 40 feet!).

Argentinosaurus Stats

Period: Late Cretaceous
Average Height: 70 feet
Average Length: 98-130 feet
Average Weight: 80-100 tons
Diet: Herbivore
Roamed: Argentina
Speed of about: 5 mph or less

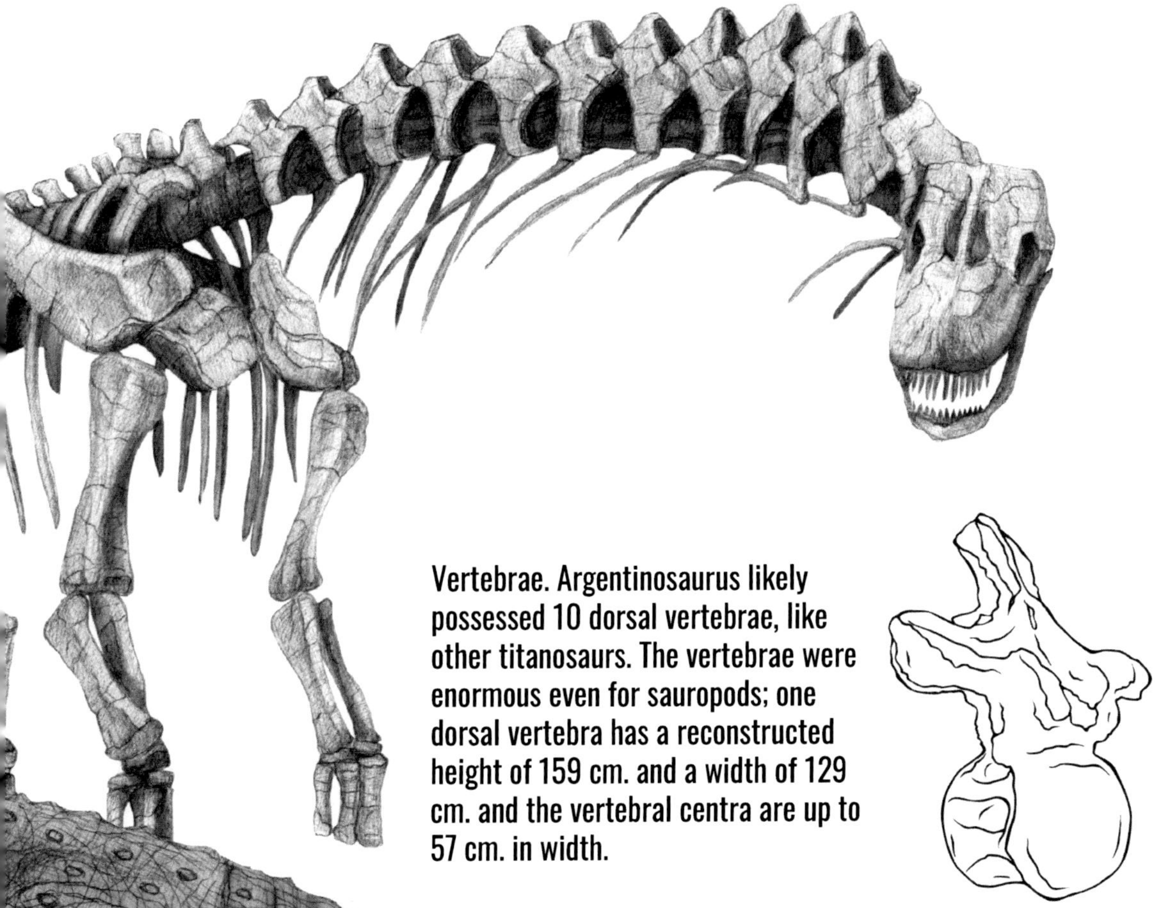

ARGENTINOSAURUS

Vertebrae. Argentinosaurus likely possessed 10 dorsal vertebrae, like other titanosaurs. The vertebrae were enormous even for sauropods; one dorsal vertebra has a reconstructed height of 159 cm. and a width of 129 cm. and the vertebral centra are up to 57 cm. in width.

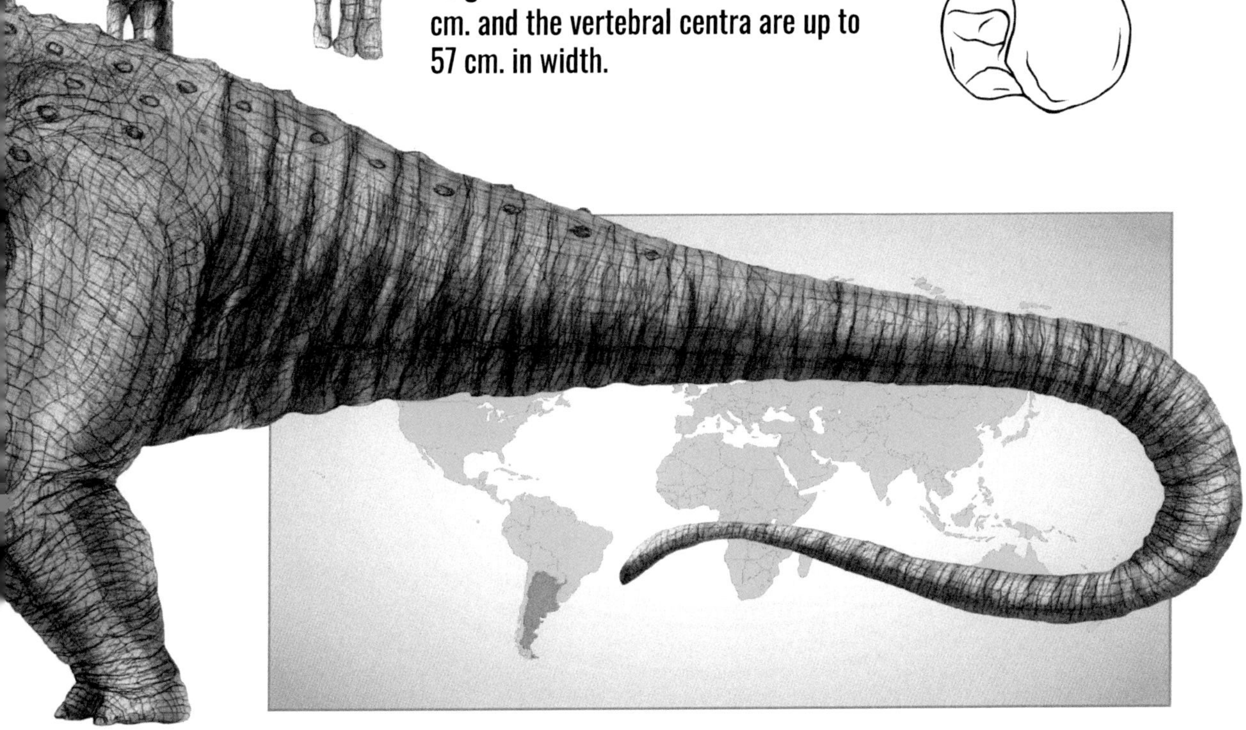

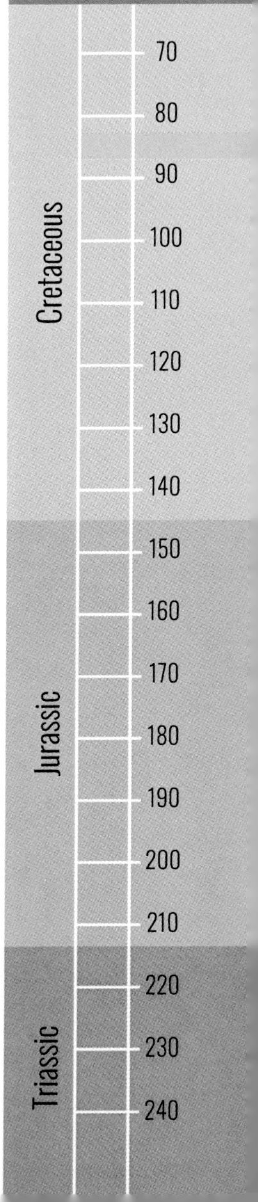

Cretaceous
Jurassic
Triassic

70
80
90
100
110
120
130
140
150
160
170
180
190
200
210
220
230
240

SPINOSAURUS

Spinosaurus, which translates to "spined lizard," holds the record for being the longest land carnivore ever known! It's in the same league as big predators like Tyrannosaurus, Giganotosaurus, and Carcharodontosaurus. Spinosaurus had a varied diet, munching on fish and likely hunting both on land and in water. Scientists think it might have been a good swimmer, but that's still up for debate.

What's interesting is its leg bones were super dense, helping it stay afloat in the water. That big sail on its back? Some think it helped regulate its body temperature, while others say it was for showing off to friends or potential mates.

Spinosaurus lived in a lush, watery world filled with all sorts of dinosaurs, fish, crocodiles, lizards, turtles, pterosaurs, and even plesiosaurs. Talk about a diverse neighborhood!

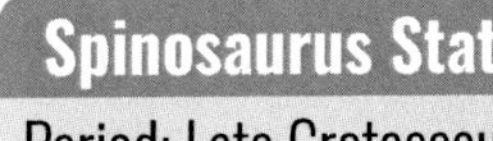

Spinosaurus Stats

Period: Late Cretaceous
Average Height: 16-20 feet
Average Length: 40-48 feet
Average Weight: 12-19 tons
Diet: Carnivore (Piscivore)
Roamed: North Africa, Egypt and Morocco
Speed of about: 24-34 mph

SPINOSAURUS

Fun Facts about the Spinosaurus

1. Given the fact that the Spinosaurus lived in lush, watery areas with plenty of fish, it was an excellent swimmer.
2. Unlike most carnivorous dinosaurs with sharp, curved teeth, Spinosaurus had powerful jaws with straight, knife-like teeth that were ideal for spearing prey. Its mouth was similar to that of a crocodile.
3. One of the most remarkable features of Spinosaurus was its enormous sail on its spine, which could reach up to seven feet in height and would rise when Spinosaurus arched its back. This sail likely served multiple purposes, including mating displays, intimidating rivals, and helping regulate the dinosaur's body temperature.

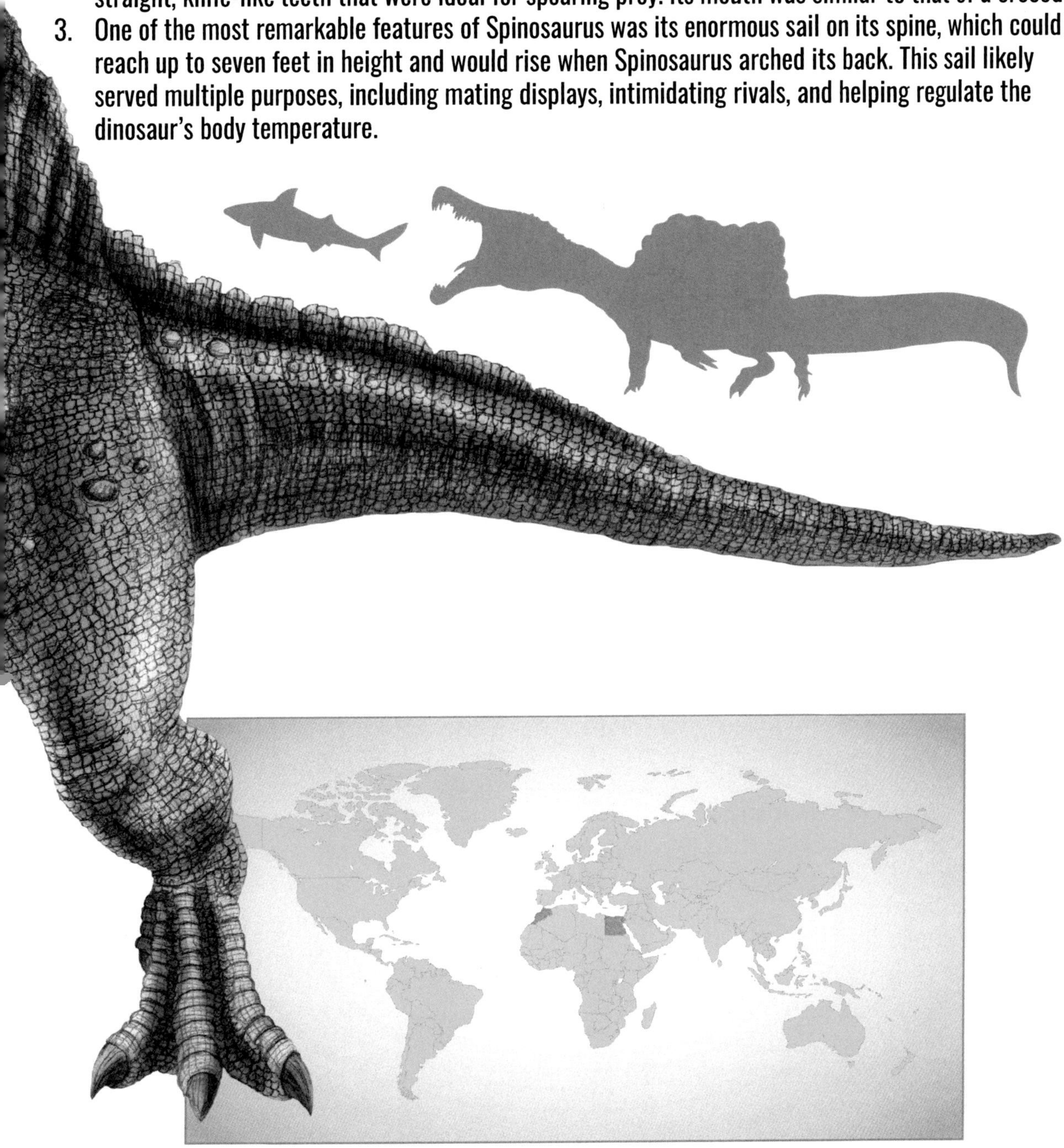

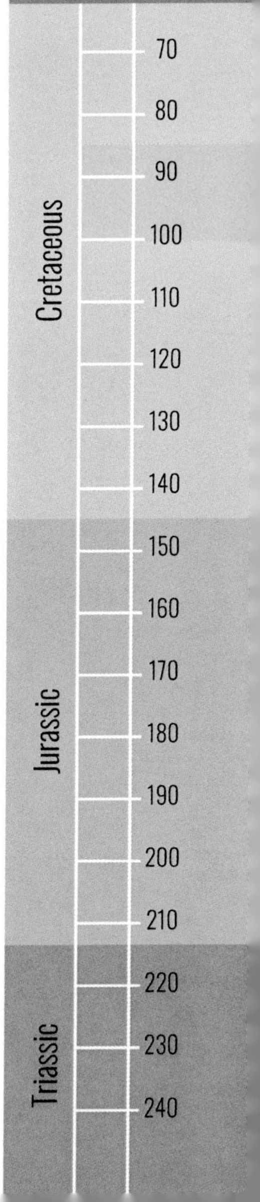

Cretaceous
Jurassic
Triassic

70
80
90
100
110
120
130
140
150
160
170
180
190
200
210
220
230
240

ELASMOSAURUS

The name Elasmosaurus translates to "thin-plate lizard," in reference to the "plate" bones of the sternal and pelvic regions of this dino. Elasmosaurus was built for life in the water, with a sleek body, paddle-like limbs, and a short tail. But its most remarkable feature was its incredibly long neck, measuring around 23 feet! Together with its relative Albertonectes, it ranked among the longest-necked animals ever, boasting an impressive 72 vertebrae in its neck, just four fewer than Albertonectes.

Its head was small and triangular, armed with large, fang-like teeth at the front and smaller ones towards the back. With six teeth in each upper jaw and possibly 14 in the lower jaw, Elasmosaurus was well-equipped for catching prey.

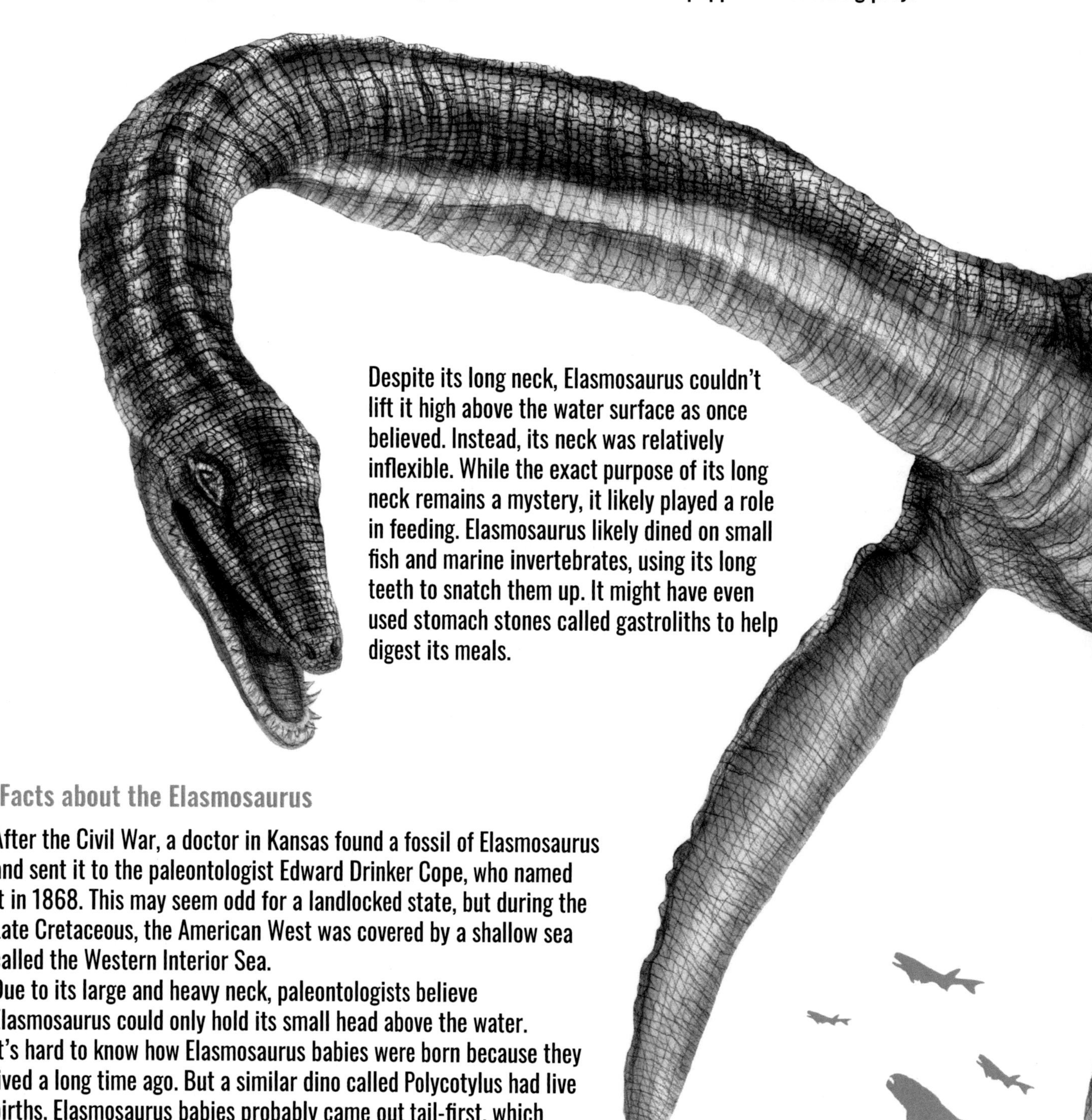

Despite its long neck, Elasmosaurus couldn't lift it high above the water surface as once believed. Instead, its neck was relatively inflexible. While the exact purpose of its long neck remains a mystery, it likely played a role in feeding. Elasmosaurus likely dined on small fish and marine invertebrates, using its long teeth to snatch them up. It might have even used stomach stones called gastroliths to help digest its meals.

Fun Facts about the Elasmosaurus

1. After the Civil War, a doctor in Kansas found a fossil of Elasmosaurus and sent it to the paleontologist Edward Drinker Cope, who named it in 1868. This may seem odd for a landlocked state, but during the Late Cretaceous, the American West was covered by a shallow sea called the Western Interior Sea.
2. Due to its large and heavy neck, paleontologists believe Elasmosaurus could only hold its small head above the water.
3. It's hard to know how Elasmosaurus babies were born because they lived a long time ago. But a similar dino called Polycotylus had live births. Elasmosaurus babies probably came out tail-first, which helped them get used to living underwater.

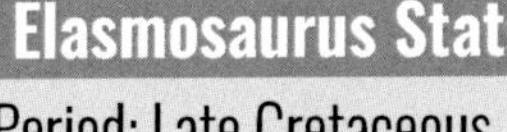

Elasmosaurus Stats

Period: Late Cretaceous
Average Height: 45 feet
Average Length: 30-40 feet
Average Weight: 11-15 tons
Diet: Carnivore (Piscivore)
Roamed: North America
Speed of about: Around 5 mph

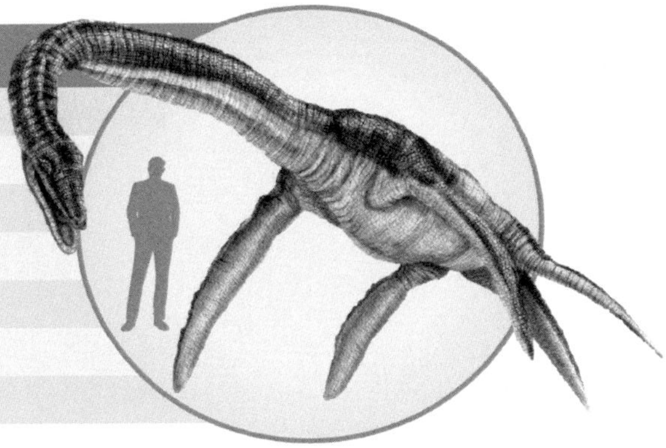

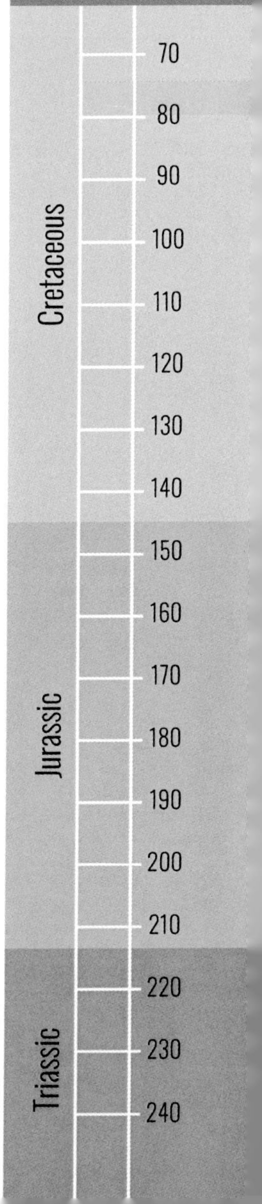

ELASMOSAURUS

Period	Million years ago
Cretaceous	70, 80, 90, 100, 110, 120, 130, 140
Jurassic	150, 160, 170, 180, 190, 200, 210
Triassic	220, 230, 240

TWILIGHT OF THE DINOSAURS

A long time ago, there were dinosaurs all over the Earth. They lived in all sorts of different shapes and sizes, changing over millions of years as the world changed around them. Some dinosaurs adapted to the changes, but others couldn't keep up and disappeared forever.

Then, about 66 million years ago, something tremendous happened. All the dinosaurs suddenly vanished, except for the ones that eventually became birds. It wasn't just dinosaurs that disappeared; many other creatures, like flying reptiles and large ocean creatures, also went extinct.

Scientists think something terrible must have happened to cause this mass extinction. Maybe a huge rock from space crashed into the Earth, or maybe there were lots of volcanic eruptions that changed the climate very quickly. Whatever it was, it happened fast, and the dinosaurs, despite being massive and powerful giants, couldn't survive it.

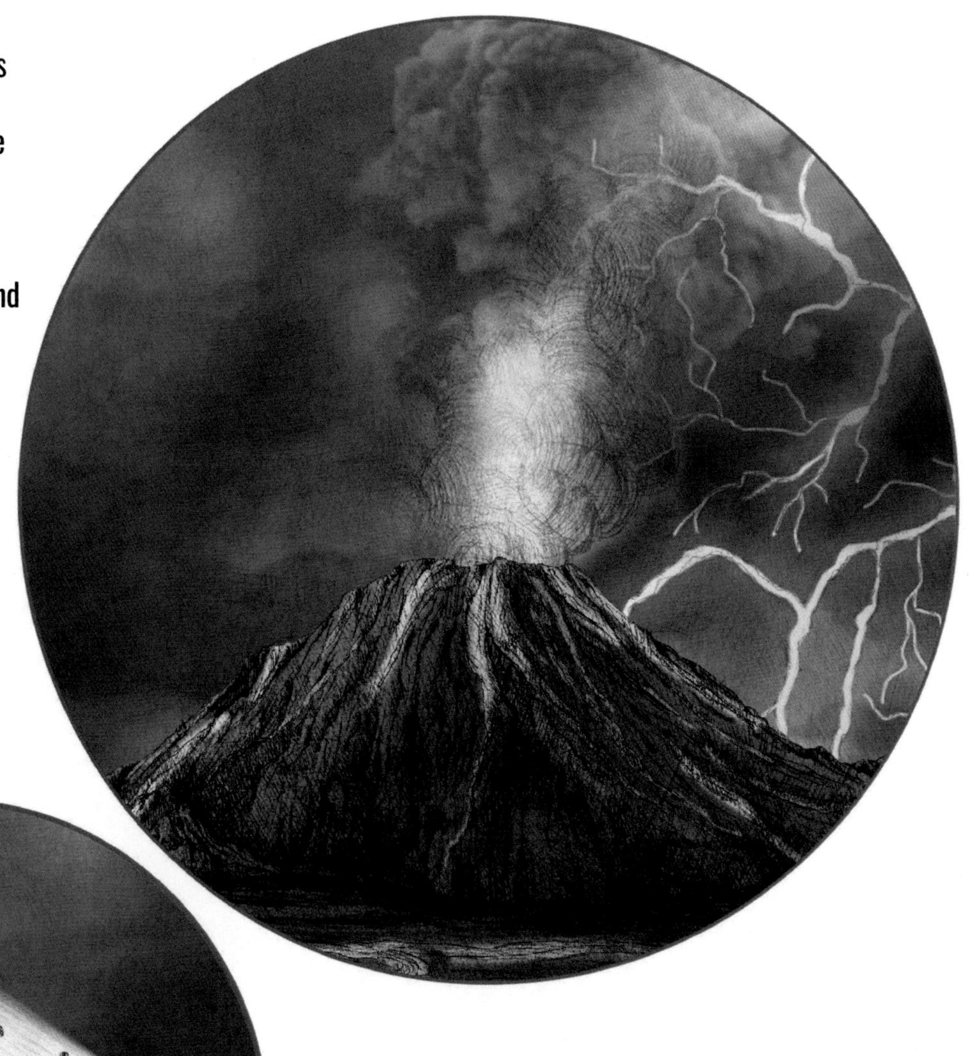

After the dinosaurs were gone, birds and mammals took over. They filled the gaps left behind by the dinos and started to change and grow in new ways. And that's how the age of the dinosaurs ended, making room for the next chapter of life on Earth.

Fun Facts!

About 66 million years ago, at the end of what scientists call the Cretaceous Period, the dinosaurs disappeared forever.

Imagine if all the time from the very start of the dinosaurs until now was squeezed into just one year on a calendar.

Picture it like this: the dinosaurs burst onto the scene on January 1st, and by the third week of September, they were gone. That's a really short time, isn't it?

Now, think about this: if the Earth formed about 18.5 years before the dinosaurs showed up, that means it took a really, really long time for everything to get ready for them!

But guess what? We humans, Homo sapiens, didn't even arrive until the very last moments of this imaginary year—right before midnight on December 31st, just in time for New Year's Eve!

Even though the dinosaurs didn't stick around forever, they were definitely superstars in Earth's history. They were the kings and queens of the land for such a long time!

EXTINCTION AND BEYOND

Dinosaurs ruled the Earth for about 230 million years, but around 66 million years ago, they suddenly disappeared along with other creatures like marine reptiles and flying reptiles. This extinction event wiped out about three-quarters of life on Earth.

There are two main ideas about what caused this extinction. Some people think a giant space rock called a meteor crashed into the Earth. This could have caused the weather to change a lot because there was so much dust in the air.

Experts also found a special metal called iridium in rocks from that time which backs up the meteor idea. Also, there's a big hole in Mexico called Chicxulub that matches the believed size of the giant space rock, and it's estimated to have crashed on Earth during the same time scientists believe the dinos disappeared.

Some people think something else caused the animals to disappear. They say there were lots of enormous volcanoes in India that may have erupted. This could have sent lots of smoke and gas into the sky, altering the weather a lot.

Some scientists think maybe both events happened together. They believe the volcanoes made the animals weak, so when the space rock hit, it was even harder for them to survive.

What do you think?

LIFE AFTER DINOSAURS

When big dinosaurs that couldn't fly disappeared 66 million years ago, Earth didn't have many large plant-eating animals for 25 million years. Scientists wondered how this affected plants and animals.

Back then, palm trees had big fruits and were covered in sharp thorns. But when the big plant-eaters were gone, fewer new palm trees with small fruits showed up. The big ones stayed the same. Even after the dinosaurs were gone, palm fruits kept getting bigger. This meant smaller animals could still eat them and spread their seeds.

Without big plant-eaters, plants with bigger seeds and fruits grew more. But they didn't need sharp things like thorns anymore because there weren't many predators. When new big plant-eaters came later, the sharp stuff came back on most palm trees. But the changes in fruit size stayed.

It's incredible to think about how plants changed when big plant-eaters disappeared and came back. This helps us guess what might happen in the future. If big animals disappear now because of people and the weather, it could change how plants grow and how animals spread seeds.

After the dinosaurs and flying reptiles were gone, mammals and birds started to take over on land. But what about the oceans?

Well, something interesting happened. In the first 10 million years after the dinosaurs disappeared, five big groups of fish called acanthomorphs showed up, along with other sea creatures. These acanthomorphs include fish we know, like tunas, cods, and pufferfishes. Now, they make up about a third of all animals with backbones!

The surprising thing is that all these different kinds of fish appeared right after the big extinction 66 million years ago. It's like they got a special chance to grow and become various kinds of fish super fast.

In the future, scientists want to learn even more about fish by studying their genes. This can help us understand how they changed over time, especially compared to mammals and birds.

A DINOSAUR-SIZED LEGACY

Dinosaurs have left a significant mark on our world, even though they lived millions of years ago. They've left behind lots of cool stuff that helps us learn about them and our planet:

Fossils: Dinosaurs left behind many fossils, which are like clues from the past. Scientists use these fossils to learn about how dinosaurs looked, behaved, and lived together. By studying them, scientists can figure out what Earth was like a long time ago.

Scientific Discoveries: Dinosaurs have helped scientists make many important discoveries. They've shown us how animals changed over time, like how some dinosaurs evolved into birds. Also, studying dinosaur fossils has helped scientists learn about how living things work and how they fit into their environments. These discoveries teach us not just about dinosaurs but also about science in general.

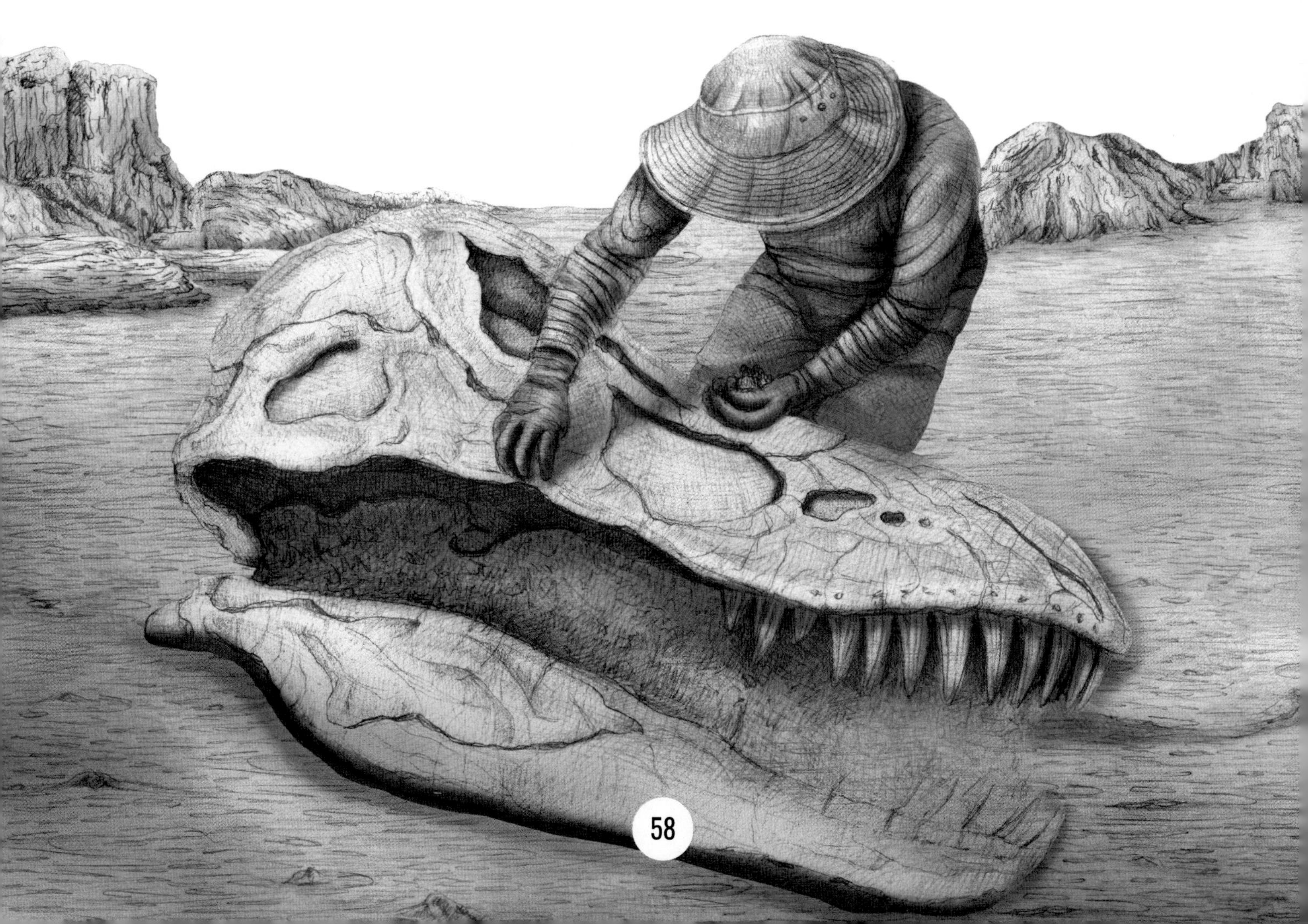

Inspiration for Innovation: Dinosaurs are super exciting and have inspired lots of people to come up with new and awesome things. Scientists, artists, writers, and moviemakers love dinosaurs because they're so unique and interesting. They've helped create realistic dinosaur models and cool tools for studying fossils.

Education and Outreach: Dinosaurs are great teachers! They're in museums, books, and movies, making learning about science really fun. People of all ages love dinosaurs, and they help us learn about the world around us. By getting kids interested in dinosaurs, they might become scientists when they grow up!

Cultural Impact: Dinosaurs are everywhere in stories! They're in books, movies, and games, making them famous around the world. People love dinosaurs so much that they're in stories from long ago and stories from different countries. They're a big part of our culture and imagination.

Overall, dinosaurs have had a BIG impact on how we live our lives today! They've helped us learn a lot about nature, sparked new ideas in science, fired up our imagination, and become a big part of our culture and society.

Made in the USA
Monee, IL
17 December 2024